The WONDER OF ADVENT

DELIGHTING IN THE HOPE, JOY,
PEACE, AND LOVE OF CHRISTMAS

LIFEWAY WOMEN

With Music by ADRIENNE CAMP

Lifeway Press®
Brentwood, Tennessee

Published by Lifeway Press® • © 2022 Lifeway Christian Resources • Brentwood, TN

ISBN: 978-1-0877-5881-7
Item: 005836522
Dewey decimal classification: 232.92
Subject headings: ADVENT / JESUS CHRIST--NATIVITY / HOPE

To order additional copies of this resource, write to Lifeway Resources Customer Service; 200 Powell Place, Suite 100, Brentwood, TN 37027-7514; order online at www.lifeway.com; fax 615.251.5933; phone toll free 800.458.2772; or email orderentry@lifeway.com.

Printed in the United States of America

Lifeway Women Bible Studies • Lifeway Resources •
200 Powell Place, Suite 100, Brentwood, TN 37027-7514

EDITORIAL TEAM, LIFEWAY WOMEN BIBLE STUDIES

Becky Loyd
Director, Lifeway Women

Tina Boesch
Manager, Lifeway Women Bible Studies

Chelsea Waack
Production Leader

Laura Magness
Content Editor

Tessa Morrell
Production Editor

Lauren Ervin
Graphic Designer

Contents

How to use this study

WATCH

Each video features music from Adrienne Camp; an Advent-themed Scripture reading and candle lighting; and a brief teaching time. Watch the video at the start of your week, before you do the personal Bible study, and take notes on the *WATCH* pages.

DISCUSS

Each session includes a *DISCUSS* page. If you are part of a *The Wonder of Advent* Bible study group, this is where you can take notes during your group time and jot down any prayer requests mentioned.

PERSONAL STUDY

You'll study everything from Old Testament prophecies about Jesus to specific moments in the Christmas story and Jesus's time on earth. You'll even get to look ahead to some of the promises about His return. It's a lot to cover, so stretch your study out over seven days if you need to.

ACTIVITIES

Christmas is one of the best times of the year to share the love of Jesus with others. The *ACTIVITIES* that accompany each session are designed to be Christmas-y and fun, but more importantly, they will help you open the door to those conversations.

SUGGESTED SCHEDULE

Welcome! We're so glad you've picked up this book. Advent is a truly WONDERful time of year, a time when Christians around the world are focused together on the birth of Jesus and the promise that He will come again. The themes of Advent are timeless, but if you prefer to follow a more "traditional" Advent schedule, it's helpful to know that Advent begins four Sundays out from Christmas, on the Sunday that falls between November 27 and December 3.

FIRST SUNDAY OF ADVENT — Watch the video "Session One: Hope" and light the first Advent candle (see "Advent Wreath," page 164). Then read the Week One personal study during the week.

SECOND SUNDAY OF ADVENT — Watch the video "Session Two: Joy" and light the second Advent candle. Then read the Week Two personal study during the week.

THIRD SUNDAY OF ADVENT — Watch the video "Session Three: Peace" and light the third Advent candle. Then read the Week Three personal study during the week.

FOURTH SUNDAY OF ADVENT — Watch the video "Session Four: Love" and light the fourth Advent candle. Then read the Week Four personal study during the week.

Regardless of when you study, our hope is that you will adopt an Advent mindset of wonder and expectation that lasts year round.

LEADING A GROUP?

Thank you for leading a group through *The Wonder of Advent*! Here is a list of tools to help you lead.

LEADER GUIDE (pages 168–173) to help you structure each group meeting and facilitate small group discussion

DEVOTIONAL VIDEOS to watch together at each group session. You'll find detailed information for how to access the teaching videos that accompany this study on the card inserted in the back of your Bible study book.

FREE DOWNLOADS to help you promote the study in your church or neighborhood, including: invitation card, promotional poster, bulletin insert, and PowerPoint® template. You'll find these and more at lifeway.com/wonder.

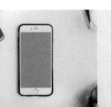
YOU'LL FIND DETAILED INFORMATION FOR HOW TO **ACCESS THE VIDEO SESSIONS** THAT ACCOMPANY THIS STUDY ON THE CARD INSERTED IN THE BACK OF YOUR BIBLE STUDY BOOK.

5

Introduction

More than any other time of year, Christmas brings an undeniable sense of wonder and awe. For some, it's the nostalgia of traditions that span generations—grandma's pie recipe, a Christmas Eve candlelight service, the same ornaments on the tree year after year. For others, it's watching the season through the eyes of a young child or simply enjoying a little less time working and a little more with family and friends.

If you're able to filter out all of the busyness, noise, and clutter and get to the heart of the season, the wonder is overpowering—God, the Creator of everything, sent His Son out of heaven and into our world to walk as we walk and live as we live. This Child, Jesus, was the rescuer God had been promising His children since everything went wrong back in the garden of Eden. God told the serpent: "He will strike your head, and you will strike his heel" (Gen. 3:15).

With Jesus's birth, God kept His word. Jesus became one of us so He could save a broken humanity from its sins. This is the good news of Christmas, but it's not the end of the story. Jesus is coming back! Advent is a celebration of both of these truths—Jesus came once, and He is coming again.

Setting aside this time of study and worship each Christmas season gives us the opportunity to delight in what we know is true in Jesus: the HOPE that He will return and make all things new; the JOY that comes from worshiping Him now and forever; the PEACE we experience with God today and we long for our world to experience when it is redeemed; and the LOVE of a God who sacrificed His own Son to be in relationship with us. These are the themes of Advent, and they fill us with wonder and awe as we reflect on our great God.

In *The Wonder of Advent*, we'll spend a week studying each of these themes. We'll look at Old Testament prophecies, scenes from the Christmas story, encounters Jesus had with people during His earthly ministry, teachings from Jesus, and promises from Revelation. When our eyes are opened to these threads in Scripture, we stand in awe of the glory and love of God and are motivated to share the wonder of Advent with the world.

Laura Magness

Hope

Yet I call this to mind, and therefore I have hope:
Because of the Lord's faithful love we do not perish,
for his mercies never end. They are new every
morning; great is your faithfulness! I say, "The Lord
is my portion, therefore I will put my hope in him."

Lamentations 3:21-24

Throughout the Old Testament, we read about how God's people longed for and hoped in God's promise of a Messiah, a ruler or "anointed one" whom God would send to bless and defend His people. In the New Testament, we read about the fulfillment of that hope—the humble birth of Jesus, God's own Son. Jesus was born into our world to restore our broken relationship with God. He would become like us, but without sin, and die for us to bring about that reconciliation.

Scripture also promises that one day Jesus will return, sin will be eradicated forever, and our broken relationship with God will be restored once and for all. We wait for that day with expectant hope because we know God keeps His promises. What a day that will be!

This week we'll look at specific promises from God and moments from the life of Jesus that teach us why our hope should rest on Him. We'll also see how we're to live until that future hope becomes our present reality. Here is where we're headed.

DAY ONE	God's promise of a Child King gave His children hope (Isa. 9:2-7).
DAY TWO	John the Baptist's birth renewed hope when things seemed hopeless (Luke 1).
DAY THREE	Jesus's power gives hope to the hopeless (Luke 7:11-17).
DAY FOUR	Jesus teaches why hope rests in Him (Luke 4:16-22).
DAY FIVE	Our hope will be fulfilled (Rev. 5).

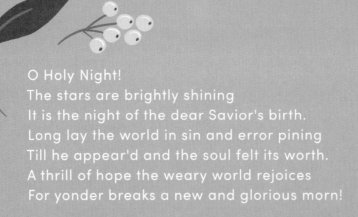

O Holy Night!
The stars are brightly shining
It is the night of the dear Savior's birth.
Long lay the world in sin and error pining
Till he appear'd and the soul felt its worth.
A thrill of hope the weary world rejoices
For yonder breaks a new and glorious morn!

Fall on your knees
Oh hear the angel voices
Oh night divine
Oh night when Christ was born
Oh night divine
Oh night divine

Truly He taught us to love one another
His law is love and His gospel is peace
Chains shall He break for the slave is our brother
And in His name all oppression shall cease
Sweet hymns of joy in grateful chorus raise we,
Let all within us praise His holy name

Christ is the Lord
O praise His Name forever
His power and glory
Evermore proclaim
His power and glory
Evermore proclaim'

WATCH THE VIDEO "Session One: Hope" (16:44) and use the space below to take notes.

HYMN: O Holy Night

SCRIPTURE READING: Isaiah 9:1-7

TO ACCESS THE VIDEO SESSIONS,
USE THE INSTRUCTIONS IN THE BACK OF YOUR BIBLE STUDY BOOK.

Discuss

If you are part of a *The Wonder of Advent* Bible study group, use this page to take notes during your group time and to keep a record of prayer requests that are mentioned.

Internal peace
Healing power
Help children to find GOD!

Day 1

A LIGHT IN THE DARKNESS
ISAIAH 9:1-7

by Kelly King

For the Northern Hemisphere, the winter solstice occurs annually on December 21 or 22. (If you live in the Southern Hemisphere, your solstice is around June 20 or 21.)[2] This is the darkest day of the year, the day with the fewest hours of sunlight, and it marks the official start to winter. We generally think of the winter solstice as an entire day, but it's really only a moment—a moment when our hemisphere is tilted as far away from the sun as it can be.

MEMORY VERSE

I say, "The LORD is my portion, therefore I will put my hope in him."

Lamentations 3:24

I'm not a fan of the dark. As a little girl, I slept with a small light on my dresser. Even though my eyes were shut, and I was fast asleep, I felt comfort knowing that no matter when I awoke, a light would be there to help me find my way. And to be honest, I still often leave a bathroom light on at night—especially when I'm traveling—because I know I might need a path to guide me in an unfamiliar room. A light keeps me from stumbling, and it overcomes the unknown of darkness.

> How do you feel about being in the dark? Consider how you feel about literal darkness, but also describe how you feel during challenging, or "dark," seasons or circumstances.

Many times throughout history, the nation of Israel experienced figurative winter solstices. Darkness seemed to be a constant companion, and wars and oppression were consistent threats. Yet, the children of God also lived with the hope that He was their light.

Read the following Old Testament passages and paraphrase what you discover about God and light.

GENESIS 1:3-5	God made light & night
EXODUS 13:21-23	He made sure the people had light. Day & night
PSALM 119:105	His word gives us light
ISAIAH 9:2	?
ISAIAH 42:6	God Gives us righteousness

God assured Israel that He was their guide, His presence provided peace, and His words illuminated their paths, no matter how dark things seemed. Beyond that, He called them to be a light in the darkness of others because of their relationship with Him.

The more you read of the Old Testament, the clearer it becomes that much of Israel's hope came through the words of God's anointed prophets (such as Jeremiah, Daniel, Ezekiel, and Hosea), most importantly their promise of Israel's future Savior. No other prophet provided a better glimpse of Israel's future Savior—the Light who would break through their darkness—than Isaiah.

READ ISAIAH 9:1-5.

The prophet Isaiah reminded God's people that a new light was coming. A child would be born whom God would raise to be a king. The reign of the coming Messiah (the promised deliverer of the Jewish nation) was seen in contrast to the reign of Ahaz, a king of Judah who rejected God and would not listen to Him. This prophecy was a source of hope for the people of Judah. They had not forgotten God's promise to King David, even though it didn't seem to be true at this time in their history.

Take a few minutes to look over God's covenant with David in 2 Samuel 7:4-17. Look specifically at verses 9 and 16. What hope for David's lineage do you see?

When David was king, God made a covenant with him. Among the promises in that covenant were that God would make a great name for David (2 Sam. 7:9), and David's kingdom would endure forever (2 Sam. 7:16). Under King Ahaz, that lineage seemed to be in danger. But in Isaiah 9, we learn about a King who was coming who would be different from all the rest.

Reread the following verses from Isaiah 9 and list the promises that are outlined in this prophecy about a future leader.

VERSE 2	The light shineth; (Jesus)
VERSE 3	Joy — Harvest
VERSE 4	Broken yoke of Burden
VERSE 5	

At the start of this prophecy, Isaiah used phrases like "a light has dawned" (v. 2), "you have enlarged the nation and increased its joy" (v. 3), and "you have shattered their oppressive yoke and the staff of their oppressor" (v. 4). These are promises of light, joy, freedom, and victory. Such words of hope for a desperate people!

Consider your current circumstances and any darkness or difficulties you might be experiencing. Which of these promises speak hope to your circumstances?

there's hope

Although our circumstances look different, we too can rest on God's promise that He is still working even when darkness seems to be engulfing us.

READ ISAIAH 9:6-7.

With these verses Isaiah continued his prophecy of a coming leader and Savior. The different imagery of this text speaks to the hope that rested on the shoulders of this King, a Child who would be born and be a light in their darkness, their lowest point, their winter solstice.

Write the four names Isaiah proclaimed about this child in Isaiah 9:6. He will be:

1. *Wonderful Counselor*
2. *mighty GOD*
3. *Everlasting Father*
4. *Prince of Peace*

These four names are sometimes considered the "throne" names—names that represent the royalty of Jesus. Unlike the personal name of Immanuel, which means God with us, these names speak to Jesus's majesty and rule over the nations. They are descriptions of a King who carries out a mission that will cause the world to marvel.

Wonderful Counselor describes a king who performs wonderful acts with the skill of wisdom. God is the source of miracles, and He is the author and embodiment of wisdom.

Mighty God captures the idea that this child would be a mighty warrior, and He would be aligned with the name of God Himself. No other king could be identified with

God in this manner. There would be something unique about this child who would bear God's name.

The third name, *Eternal Father*, is one word in Hebrew, but it combines two ideas. The ideal image of a father is one who shows compassion and love for his children. For a ruler to show compassion to a people in darkness would give Israel hope for their future. The idea that this ruler would rule forever would sound too good to be true.

The final title, *Prince of Peace*, would have easily been understood by a people who rarely experienced peace and yet longed for it. The rule of Jesus brings about wholeness and well-being to individuals and to society. Peace is about more than just the absence of war. As the Prince of Peace, Jesus accomplished everything that was required to restore a relationship between individual humans—you and me—and a holy God. Today, we still long for peace in our world (that time is coming, as we'll see in Session Three), but we can claim the peace that Jesus offers to us now when we are reunited with God through belief in His Son.

> Which of these four names describes how you need Jesus to act in your life this Advent season?
>
> Wonderful Commander

Over the next four weeks, this study will explore the themes of hope, joy, peace, and love. All four of these themes are present in this prophecy. Beyond that, Isaiah makes it clear that only through the Messiah are we able to live fully in the hope, joy, peace, and love of the Lord.

Last year, my daughter gave birth to our first grandson on December 21, the winter solstice. His name is Luken Michael. Luken is a form of Luke, which is an English form of the Latin word *lux*, meaning "light." On the darkest day of the year, Luken brought light into our family's world.

At the close of today's passage, we read, "The zeal of the LORD of Armies will accomplish this" (v. 7). In other words, God will keep His promise, and we know that He did. A baby was born to conquer the darkness of our sin. Jesus, the Light of the world, has come. ★

Day 2

A VOICE IN THE SILENCE
LUKE 1:5-25; LUKE 1:57-80

by Michelle Hicks

Not too long ago, I went through a time in my life that was unpredictable. Although I'd been able to find some hope in the past, the tsunami of problems during this particular season was overwhelming me. A car accident, cancer, surgeries, work problems, challenges with family, caring for aging parents, and that was just my personal life. Add the mega problems of the world—chaotic and toxic politics, tumultuous financial markets, and a global pandemic—and it felt like my safe places just weren't safe anymore. One thing I knew for certain: My hope was more fragile than I realized.

> Perhaps you can relate. Reflect on a time when you struggled to keep hope alive.

I imagine God's people felt much the same way in the time in their history we will study today. God's prophets had gone silent; in fact, the people hadn't heard a new word from God in four hundred years! This meant no new challenges to live for God or encouraging reminders to hope in God's promises. Not to mention the Greeks and the Romans were expanding their influence. But God had not forgotten His people or His promises to them, and fresh hope was about to come crashing through the quiet.

Read the following verses and summarize what you read in them.

Isaiah 40:3-5

Malachi 3:1

Malachi 4:5

Matthew 3:1-3

God promised to send a new prophet who would have the specific job of preparing God's people for the arrival of the Messiah. Then in Matthew 3, we see that God kept His promise through the ministry of John the Baptist. But let's back up a little bit.

READ LUKE 1:5-25.

What do you learn about Zechariah and Elizabeth's lineage and character from these verses?

	LINEAGE	CHARACTER
Zechariah		
Elizabeth		

Zechariah was a Jewish priest, a role that was passed on through family lineage. Elizabeth was a direct descendant of Aaron, the high priest and brother of Moses. These details help us understand that this couple had a strong Jewish heritage. Israel had thousands of priests at this time, and they were divided into twenty-four sections that were named for their leader (Abijah, in Zechariah's case).[3] Because there were so many, they took turns serving at the temple, and on this day the lot fell to Zechariah.

In addition to their family heritage, Luke also made a point to describe their godly character. Verse 6 reveals, "Both were righteous in God's sight, living without blame according to all the commands and requirements of the Lord." High praise for people we learn had reason to feel hopeless.

> Review Luke 1:5-25, and list four or five key details of Zechariah's experience as he served as priest on this day.

In other Gospel accounts of the birth of Jesus, an angel spoke to Mary and Joseph (Luke 1:26-38; Matt. 1:18-25). However, Luke's Gospel begins with an angel speaking to Zechariah. The angel is clear: Elizabeth will bear a son, the one who will go before the Messiah and prepare the way for Him (v. 17). This conversation between Zechariah and the angel would have taken place before Mary's or Joseph's visits from angels announcing the coming birth of Christ.

Zechariah didn't believe the angel at first. How would his wife bear a son in her old age? How could he be sure such a promise would be fulfilled (v. 18)? The angel replied, "I am Gabriel." As a devout Jew, that is a name Zechariah would recognize from the book of Daniel (Dan. 8:16; 9:21). Because he questioned God's power to work in this way, Zechariah would be mute until the promise was fulfilled as proof of the angel's visit and God's faithfulness.

After the burning of incense and the offering, it was the privilege of the priest at the evening sacrifice to bless the people who had gathered to worship at the temple. When Zechariah came out to the people, he could not speak, and they knew something miraculous had happened.

God's blessing was coming. Centuries of promises from God were about to be fulfilled. The announcement of John's birth was a source of hope for Zechariah and Elizabeth. A son was promised, and he would be the forerunner for the Messiah.

READ LUKE 1:57-80.

In these verses we see events unfold just as the angel said they would. Elizabeth gave birth to a baby boy (v. 57). Then on the eighth day of his life, the son of Zechariah and Elizabeth was circumcised, and he received his name (v. 59). For God's people, names were significant and chosen to describe the child, the parents' joy or hope, or as a sign of their faith. Gabriel had told Zechariah to name the child John (1:13), which means "Yahweh has been gracious" or "Yahweh is gracious" in Hebrew.[4] Zechariah and Elizabeth had truly experienced the graciousness of God with the birth of their son in their old age. And beyond their family, John's birth was a sign of God's grace for all His people.

Although Elizabeth had not interacted with the angel, Gabriel, she trusted Zechariah, and she demonstrated great faith as she spoke up and told her friends and neighbors that the boy would be called John. Zechariah affirmed the name, his tongue was set free, and as he was filled with the Holy Spirit, he began to speak, praising God.

READ ZECHARIAH'S PROPHECY IN LUKE 1:68-79 AGAIN.
Circle in your Bible or write in the space provided the key phrases that point to the significance of John's birth.

Like most parents, Zechariah and Elizabeth had high hopes for their son, but they had the angel's prophecy to back theirs up. John would be a prophet of God, the one who would prepare the way for Jesus's earthly ministry. Zechariah's prophecy specifically mentioned John's responsibility to teach people about salvation through forgiveness of sins and guide them into the way of peace (vv. 76-79).

How did someone prepare you to know Jesus? Spend some time reflecting on that journey and the evidence of God's pursuit of you.

Merriam-Webster defines hope as "to cherish a desire with anticipation, to want something to happen or be true."[5] It's more than an optimistic attitude. For hope to overcome despair like the things I went through, it needs to be real—as real as the pain, as strong as the grief, as powerful as the fear, or as compelling as the desire to give up. All of us have seen hope that failed to deliver. The light goes out and we find ourselves in the dark. But hope that lights up the darkness is grounded in God Himself.

> Think back to one of your darkest seasons. If you were a Christian during that time, how did God speak hope and light into your darkness? What is one way your relationship with Him changed through that season?

> Christmastime gives us many unique opportunities to share the good news of the gospel with the people in our daily lives. Think of one specific way you can share the light of Christ with another person between now and Christmas Day. If you're in a *The Wonder of Advent* Bible study group, plan to share your idea at your next group meeting so you have some extra accountability.

Christmas Cards

Remember, "The people who live in darkness have seen a great light, and for those living in the land of the shadow of death, a light has dawned" (Matt. 4:16). Jesus is the great Light to share with others. Tell others of His birth, death, and resurrection, and how hope was restored for the world. And if today you're in the midst of one of those dark seasons, keep reading, and let the truths revealed to you through your study of God's Word be a balm to your weary soul. ★

Day 3

FROM DEATH TO LIFE
LUKE 7:11-17

by Y Bonesteele

Our theme this week is *hope*, which is one of those words we use often but can be quite ambiguous. This Christmas, children may be hoping for a lot of toys. Parents may be hoping for their adult kids to come home for a family party. Someone may be hoping for a new job, new car, or restored health. We're never at a loss for things to hope in, but oftentimes our hopes aren't realized. This means the things we long for, desire, and even pray for don't come to pass. What are we to make of this? Is hope nothing more than wishful thinking? What kind of hope can we rely on and put our trust in?

From the previous two days of study, it's evident God wants us to hope, and He wants our hope to be rooted in Him and His promises. God knew His children needed something to look forward to and anchor their trust in, so He promised a Savior was coming. Then God delivered on that promise when He sent Jesus, His own Son, into the world. One of the aspects of Jesus's earthly ministry was to provide hope to the hopeless—people who were sick, paralyzed, demon possessed, poor, widowed, shamed by their community, and on and on. Today we'll look at one woman's encounter with Jesus and the hope He brought to her hopeless circumstances.

READ LUKE 7:11-14.

Fill in the first column with how you think the different people were feeling when Jesus arrived. Use the verses and your own guesses. Leave the second column for later.

PEOPLE	FEELINGS AS JESUS APPROACHED	FEELINGS AFTER THE MIRACLE
DISCIPLES AND CROWD WITH JESUS		
JESUS		
WIDOW		
WIDOW'S SON		
THE CROWD FROM THE TOWN		
THE PALLBEARERS		

Luke told the story of a time when Jesus came across a funeral procession of a woman's only son. Luke tells us she was already a widow. In the ancient middle eastern culture of Jesus's day, a widow was taken care of mainly by her male sons or sons-in-law. Not only was the woman's only son taken from her, but with him her livelihood and source of provision for all her needs. Without her son, she had no one to take care of her and no voice in her community. Surely, the mood of the funeral Jesus came upon conveyed the woman's desperation and hopelessness.

Look again at verses 11-14 and write down Jesus's two commands.

- _____ _____

- _____ _____

Luke wrote that Jesus was moved by compassion when He saw this woman in her grief. He was so moved, in fact, that He acted on her behalf. Luke included two commands from Jesus. To the widow He simply said, "Don't weep." And to her dead son He said, "Get up!" Jesus's words to the widow and her son remind us of His authority and power. Jesus, as God Himself, has the authority to change our circumstances so that we no longer have reason to weep, and He has the power to say to the dead man, rise again. He did this in Nain, and He continues to do this in our lives today.

1. Don't Weep.

Jesus encouraged the grieving mother not to weep, and then He intervened in a way that wiped away all her tears. In the book of Revelation, we read a passage that tells us a day is coming when our tears will also be no more.

> Read Revelation 21:1-4. List some of the things we get to wait and hope for.

> Why is this good news for you today? Where do you need to feel Jesus's comfort and compassion?

This is not just wishful thinking. God promises this day to us, and we know from the testimony of God's Word that He keeps His promises. One day, we will be with Jesus face to face, and all sorrow will cease to exist. Let this truth be a source of hope and comfort for you this Advent season.

2. Get Up!

After comforting the mother (v. 13), Jesus "touched the open coffin" and said, "Young man, I tell you, get up!" (v. 14). In this story, He restored life to a dead man and restored hope to his mother. Jesus brought honor back to the family when only shame was on the horizon.

READ EPHESIANS 2:1-5. In your own words, summarize the resurrection Paul describes in these verses.

In the story of our lives, Jesus also offers restoration. In Ephesians 2, Paul uses the death to life imagery to describe who a person is before meeting Jesus and how in Christ a person is made new. We were once dead to our sin, guilt, and shame, but through a relationship with Jesus we are alive. And this new life is all because of His sacrificial work on the cross to die for our sins. In Christ we can have true hope in life everlasting, and we can point others toward the hope that is found in Him as well.

READ LUKE 7:15-17.

Now, fill out the second column in the chart on page 28 with what you think the people felt after Jesus's miracle. Use the verses to help you answer.

Jesus had gained a following, in part, because of the miracles and healings He performed. This was one of three times Jesus raised someone from the dead. The response of the crowd was one of fear mixed with awe, an appropriate response. When we see life change in someone who has chosen to follow Jesus, or when we see everyday provisions God graces us with, we should also respond by glorifying God.

What did the crowd decide about Jesus because of this miracle? In what sense were they right? In what sense were they wrong?

The crowd at Nain knew they had witnessed a miracle, something only God had the authority to do. However, in the end they failed to see who Jesus really is. They thought Jesus was a prophet sent by God. The crowds had not yet figured out that Jesus was truly God Himself.

Look closely, and you'll see yourself in the crowd. Even in knowing Jesus, we forget what His true mission and purpose is. His mission isn't to make us happy people in this world (although we do find joy in Him), and it isn't to make us moral people (although we do live more rightly because of Christ). It isn't even so we can have a holiday at the end of the year to celebrate Him and give and receive presents (although that's an added bonus). Jesus's mission is to seek and save the lost (Luke 19:10), so that we might have a relationship with God that lasts forever.

> What are you hoping for this next year? Do you trust that God is sovereign over it, even if it doesn't come to fruition?

> List some things you can find hope in that you know will come to pass because of Jesus Christ.

When we talk about Jesus being our hope, it's not hope in having Him grant our wishes or desires. It's hope in Jesus Himself, who walks alongside us in this life to carry our burdens, take away our guilt and shame, wipe every tear, give us new life, and help us to live with passion, faith, and love while we wait for our promised forever. Take some time now to thank God for that hope. ★

Day 4

FOREVER FREEDOM
LUKE 4:14-30

by Ashley Marivittori Gorman

Before you begin today's study, take a few minutes to think through the following question to put yourself in the scene we enter in Luke 4.

What do you imagine it would have been like to hear Jesus teach in a synagogue?

READ LUKE 4:14-16.

Luke tells readers that "as usual" (v. 16), Jesus was teaching in many synagogues throughout the region of Galilee. When His travels brought Him back to His hometown of Nazareth, He followed suit. And He is welcomed—at first.

We learn some important details about the early days of Jesus's public ministry from these few verses. That Jesus would read and expound Scripture in a synagogue setting is an important detail. Instead of viewing Jesus as an ordinary guy in the shadows pulling off a covert mission that only His disciples knew about, the truth is, the whole region of Galilee considered Him a traveling Rabbi, a Jewish teacher. Visiting Rabbis were often the ones who would read the scroll during synagogue worship.

Why is it important for us to realize that Jesus was considered a Rabbi in His day?

Jewish Teacher

In Jesus's day, synagogue worship followed a protocol where an attendant would hand the reader an assigned book from Scripture, the reader would stand to read it, and then he would sit to comment on it. In God's divine providence, Isaiah was the chosen scroll that landed in Jesus's palm, and Jesus intentionally chose a passage within it to reveal something else that was chosen—namely, Himself.

READ ISAIAH 61:1-2 (LUKE 4:18-19), and list everything Jesus revealed about His ministry and purpose.

As Jesus spoke the words of Isaiah 61:1-2, He reminded His listeners about their coming Anointed One. Someone who would proclaim good news to the poor, bind up broken hearts, free trapped captives, open the eyes of the blind, comfort those who mourn, and declare a time of God's favor (vv. 18-19). These phrases drip with terminology related to the Year of Jubilee, which God mandated as part of His laws for the Israelites in Leviticus 25:

> "You are to consecrate the fiftieth year and proclaim freedom in the land for all its inhabitants. It will be your Jubilee, when each of you is to return to his property and each of you to his clan. . . . It is to be holy to you because it is the Jubilee" (Lev. 25:10-12).

In Jewish law, the Jubilee occurred every fifty years and operated as a cultural "reset" where all of life returned to a state of freedom and rest. Slaves were freed to return to their communities. Those in bondage and indebtedness were released from chains and debt alike. Even the land was given rest from its toil. The picture here is widespread redemption and restoration—the world gaining some semblance of the way it was always supposed to be before sin broke everything. The concept of Jubilee sings of hope for the hopeless.

After Jesus was done speaking, He rolled up the scroll, handed it back to the attendant, and sat down to find everyone's eyes intently fixed on Him, signaling that it was time for the Rabbi to give insight on the passage. And insight is exactly what Jesus gave: "Today as you listen, this Scripture has been fulfilled" (v. 21).

Today? Such immediacy would have surprised Jesus's listeners, for they knew this passage in Isaiah could only be fulfilled in the messianic era. Jesus, sitting there before them, is the Appointed One who would usher in hope for the hopeless. The Child King Isaiah promised them in Isaiah 9, the Redeemer heralded by John the Baptist (Luke 3:1-6). Through Jesus, the reality of Jubilee would extend over God's people eternally. They would be freed forever from the dominion of not just physical slavery but spiritual slavery to sin. They would not be simply healed of this or that illness in their lifetime, but forevermore healed from death itself by means of resurrection life. This was the good news He proclaimed: that the hope of a forever-Jubilee had come. And it was found in Jesus Himself.

> List some ways the "forever-Jubilee" that is ours through Jesus is different from the "50-year Jubilee" practiced in the law.

"Not his Child"
Bau
Song from

After hearing these words, the people's response was mixed (v. 22). Among the chatter was praise to Jesus for His "gracious words." After all, who doesn't want freedom and rest? But that was only part of the response.

> Why do you think it was hard for Jesus's audience in Luke 4 to take Him seriously (v. 22)?

Remember, Jesus was teaching in His own (tiny) hometown. Nazareth, according to some scholars, is said to have been inhabited by fewer than five hundred people.[6] These people didn't merely see Him as a wise itinerant teacher. They knew Him; they had watched Him grow from childhood. Wait a minute; isn't this Jesus, the carpenter's son? Where did He get the authority to tell us the Messianic Age is here or that He'd be the one to usher it in?

READ LUKE 4:23-30.

Jesus could sense the unbelief swirling inside His fellow Nazarenes and discerned the earthly logic building in their minds. Given the customary nature of debate during this part of the worship service, He knew they would want Him to prove what He just said, and He anticipated their rebuttal: Surely this carpenter's son is just bluffing. If He's really ushering in the messianic age, then He should prove it by performing the miracles here that rumor says He's performed in other towns (v. 23).

And Jesus's response? "No prophet is accepted in his hometown" (v. 24). The people of God had a historical habit of rejecting their own prophets like Elijah and Elisha. After all, Jesus argued, it was a widow from Zarephath who got the miracle of bread amidst famine, not the widows of Israel (1 Kings 17). And of all the lepers in Israel, only Naaman the Syrian was healed (2 Kings 5). Gentiles. Jubilee for Gentiles! This was the plan of God all along—to bring forth a Savior from the Jews who would also include the Gentiles in His global plans of hope and healing.

As you can imagine, this news didn't go over well with an entirely Jewish gathering—to the point that the people in Jesus's hometown ran Him out of town and attempted to throw Him off a cliff (v. 29)! The thought that God has a plan beyond just my people group and that His offer of Jubilee extends to people who aren't like me—this was too much for Jesus's listeners to bear. They hated the idea that their hearts could be in the wrong place. That on a spiritual level, they were possibly blind and sick. That the pagan "others" might get the perks of their Messiah. And I wonder, are we guilty of the same kind of thinking?

> Be honest with yourself: Who is "them" for you? Who do you bristle against, believing "they" don't deserve a chance at gospel hope? What does this inclination say about the type of character you'd be if you found yourself in the story of Luke 4?

Jesus came to free them and you and me and anyone who might believe in His ability to break the bonds of sin and death. But to experience the chains broken off, we must admit they are there. To enjoy the sweet relief of healing, we must admit we're sick.

To recover our sight, we must admit we're blind. Most of Jesus's synagogue listeners bristled at this. They just couldn't do it. Jubilee sounded nice, of course, but they couldn't bring themselves to admit they needed it. And so, for all the hope dangling in front of them—theirs for the taking—they swatted it away.

Well, not all of them. A small few believed Jesus. To them, He granted immediate healing as a signpost for the future healing that awaits all who trust in His eternal promise to defeat sin and death forever (Mark 6:4-6).

So, what about you? Are you a home-towner who doubts or an outsider who believes? Because here's the truth: Jesus has offered gospel hope for the hopeless. Have you truly taken hold of the Jubilee Jesus offers you?

If you're a Christian, in what ways have you forgotten the Jubilee that Jesus has granted you? In what ways are you living like it's not real?

In what practical ways can you live like the Jubilee Jesus offers is real and true? How does that change the way you live today? Your attitude toward others? Your hope for the future? ★

Day 5

OUR FUTURE HOPE
REVELATION 5

by Tessa Morrell

The world has felt particularly broken to me over the last few years. We've endured an ongoing global pandemic that has taken countless lives, changed day-to-day life as we know it, and created divisions among large groups of people and even families and friends.

In addition to the collective weight of grief and pain, we've also experienced the normal ups and downs of life that come from existing in a world that is broken by sin—illness, disappointment, death, loss, loneliness, and pain.

Romans 8 describes the groaning weight of sin and decay that even the very fabric of creation experiences. In verse 22, the apostle Paul describes the pain of this brokenness as labor pains, which really is the perfect imagery. With labor pains comes the anticipation that they will eventually end, and new life will be waiting on the other side.

That's where we find ourselves today—waiting and hurting and wondering when the suffering will stop. The dark days may feel long right now, but there is always hope and, as we've seen this week, that hope is found in Jesus. He was born, He lived a perfect life, He died as a sacrifice for sin, and He overcame death once and for all by rising from the grave.

Now, Jesus sits at the right hand of the Father and promises us that He is coming back for us soon. For our final text this week, we look at one more promise God gives us— the future hope that when Jesus returns, He will put an end to our labor pains once and for all.

READ REVELATION 5:1-7.

Descriptions we read in Scripture of heaven and the glory of God are overwhelming. To help paint a picture in your mind of the scene described in these verses, list some of the things you notice. Who is mentioned? What actions are described? Write what you see here.

Why do you think John wept when no one was found worthy to open the scroll (v. 4)?

At the root of sin and separation from God is the reality that no matter what a person does, thinks, feels, or desires, it can never be good enough to save her from sin and brokenness. Without Christ, humanity is completely without hope. And when this reality registers deep in a person's soul—the understanding that there is *nothing* a person can do to take control and fix the overbearing weight of sin and suffering—it's devastating.

The scroll described in these verses contained God's final judgments, and it symbolized the authority and power of God. The seal on it, like the wax seal that bound an important document, could only be opened by a person of great authority. John felt helpless and hopeless when he realized that no one present was worthy to break that seal and read the words the scroll contained.

And then John saw Jesus—the Lamb who was slain for the forgiveness of sin and the only One who has the power and authority to bring about redemption. Colossians 1:15 tells us that Jesus "is the image of the invisible God, the firstborn over all creation." Jesus is fully God, and He became fully human when He was born on this earth so that He could one day die to pay the price for our sins (Rom. 6:23). That victory over sin and death gave Jesus the authority to read and act on the scroll's words of judgment and redemption.

READ ISAIAH 53:7 AND JOHN 1:29. What is the significance of these verses and the description of Jesus as the "lamb" in Revelation 5:6-7?

Throughout the Old Testament, the lamb is commonly linked to animal sacrifices given to God to atone for sin. In Isaiah 53:7, the prophet Isaiah used the imagery of a sacrificial lamb to look forward to the sacrifice of the Suffering Servant, the Messiah. In John 1:29, John the Baptist connects these two threads when he refers to Jesus as "the Lamb of God, who takes away the sin of the world."

READ REVELATION 5:8-10.

What was the reaction of every creature and elder when the Lamb took hold of the scroll?

Sing a new song!

What are some of the highlights of the new song they sang in verses 9-10? Summarize the song in a few statements.

The creatures and the elders fell in worship before the Lamb when they witnessed His power and authority. They sang that He is worthy to take the scroll—to take the plans of God and reveal them. He is the Lamb who was slaughtered for the sins of the people, purchasing those who place their faith in Jesus and welcoming them into His family.

Jesus makes believers a family—a kingdom filled with people from every tribe, tongue, people, and nation. In his letter to the Ephesians, the apostle Paul explains that unity is a key aspect of the family of God. Through Jesus, all who believe in Him are brought near by His blood; because of the Lamb, we are no longer foreigners and strangers, but members of God's family (Eph. 2:13,19).

Why is it important for us to remember that God's kingdom is made up of a diverse group of believers?

READ REVELATION 5:11-14.

Try to imagine the overpowering roar of voices filling the heavens and proclaiming the glory of Jesus. It's almost unfathomable, isn't it? Verse 13 tells us that every creature in heaven, on earth, under the earth, on the sea, and everything in them worshiped the Lamb. The One who gave His life for our redemption receives all the glory and praise for all eternity.

> In the space below, write a prayer of worship to Jesus, the Lamb of God who was promised, who came, and who died and rose again to provide the gift of salvation. In your prayer, incorporate some of the language John recorded from the worship of the creatures and elders.

As we navigate this tension of living in the hurting but hopeful time in history that we find ourselves in, it helps to remember that this broken world is exactly where Jesus chose to dwell. He came close to us in our brokenness so that we could be made whole in Him. God sent His beloved Son—the Messiah who was promised for centuries before His birth in Bethlehem—to be near to us and to provide hope, peace, and His presence even in the darkest night.

Yes, this world is broken. But we have a Savior who is greater than any pain, suffering, and sickness we endure in this life. And even better, we have the promise of the second advent of Jesus when He will return to earth and call His people home. He will establish His kingdom in a new heaven and earth, and all the brokenness and pain we endure now will be a distant memory as we live peacefully with Him for eternity. He is worthy of all praise and honor as we anticipate that beautiful day. ★

HOW TO MAKE GINGERBREAD MEN COOKIES

by Chelsea Waack

When shops are bustling and our Christmas to-do lists seem never ending, we must be intentional about taking time to slow down and dwell in the hope of the Advent season. Baking is always a great way to push pause. These gingerbread men cookies are a sweet reminder that God sent His Son for all people. Bake up a batch to share with others in anticipation of Jesus's birth.

SUPPLIES

- 1 tablespoon baking powder
- 1 teaspoon ground cloves
- 1 teaspoon ground cinnamon
- 1 tablespoon ground ginger
- 1 teaspoon ground nutmeg
- 6 cups all-purpose flour
- 1 cup packed brown sugar
- 1 egg
- 1 cup molasses
- 1 cup shortening, melted and cooled slightly
- 1 teaspoon vanilla extract
- ½ cup water

DIRECTIONS

1. Sift together the dry ingredients: baking powder, ginger, nutmeg, cloves, cinnamon, and flour.

2. In another bowl, mix the brown sugar, egg, molasses, shortening, vanilla, and water. Stir in the dry ingredients, until they are absorbed. Take the dough and divide it into 3 pieces, patting each piece down to 1 1/2 inches thick. Then wrap each piece in plastic wrap before refrigerating them for 3 hours.

3. Preheat the oven to 350 degrees fahrenheit. Lightly flour your workspace, then roll the dough out to 1/4 inch thickness. Use your favorite cookie cutters, and place cut cookies onto an ungreased cookie sheet one inch apart.

4. Bake for 10 to 12 minutes. When the cookies are baked, they will be soft to the touch. Allow the cookies to cool on wire racks. Once cool, you can decorate your cookies however you like![7]

SONGS OF HOPE

by Brooke Hill

The Old Testament is filled with a lot of "one days." One day, Abraham and Sarah would have a baby (Gen. 15). One day, God's people would be free of slavery and Egypt (Ex. 3). One day, a child would be born, and through Him, God would save the world (Isa. 9).

Sometimes, God's timing doesn't feel very convenient to us. Especially in our instant gratification, order-anything-in-minutes and talk-to-anyone-in-seconds technology-based society, we are not used to having to wait for things. Patience is hard, and there's certainly a reason that it's a fruit of the Spirit (Gal. 5:22).

Yet, Peter tells us, "With the Lord one day is like a thousand years, and a thousand years like one day. The Lord does not delay his promise, as some understand delay, but is patient with you" (2 Pet. 3:8-9). We have hope readily available to us because we know that the Lord does not delay His promise, even when our feelings don't align with that truth.

The Psalms are filled with songs of people proclaiming praises because of the hope they have found in God. Psalm 27 declares, "I am certain that I will see the LORD's goodness . . . Wait for the LORD" (vv. 13-14). What is the "one day" that you've been praying for your teen? Whether it's for them to start caring about their grades, to use kinder words, to break free of that bad habit, or for them to come to know the Lord, it can be so hard to trust that God's timing is

infinitely better than ours if we're not actively reminding ourselves of the hope God has promised through Jesus.

ACTIVITY

Music has a way of helping us express laments and praises we otherwise can't find words for.

Make a joint playlist with your teen and add songs that bring you hope. Find some songs that make your heart excited for what's to come and help you trust God's promises.

Talk with your teen about why the songs you chose give you hope and ask them to share why the songs they chose give them hope.

If you and your teen are feeling extra creative, write your own psalm of praise to sing or pray to the Lord when you're in need of hope. When either one of you is having a hard time trusting in God's promises, come back to this playlist and listen to songs of hope.

A THREAD RUNNING THROUGH IT

by Bekah Stoneking

The Bible is a huge book. It's full of many true stories that fit together to tell the one big story of God and His people.

There is a thread that runs through all of these stories. Not an actual piece of thread or string, but a common, consistent theme that connects the stories—Jesus.

The stories in the Old Testament books tell about God's holiness, people's sinfulness, and God's plan to send a Messiah to rescue us. The New Testament tells us about Jesus the Messiah. In the person of Jesus, God became a human like you and me. But Jesus lived a perfect, sinless life, died on the cross as a sacrifice for sin, and rose again on the third day.

But the story doesn't end there. The New Testament also tells us that one day, Jesus will return and make all things new!

The arrival of Jesus the Messiah is evidence of God's faithfulness. And because we know God always keeps His promises, we can confidently hope in Jesus and look forward with excitement to His return.

SUPPLIES

Gather some cardboard tubes—like from an empty roll of paper towels or wrapping paper—some glue or tape, different colors of yarn, and a pair of scissors.

DIRECTIONS

1. Cut the cardboard tube into 1-2" thick slices, then make one cut through each slice to create a cuff bracelet.

2. Use some glue or tape to secure the end of a long piece of yarn along the edge of your cardboard bracelet. Wrap the yarn around and around your bracelet until it is covered. Secure the end of the yarn with more glue or tape.

3. Next, wrap a piece of tape around the end of a differently-colored piece of yarn. Weave the taped end of that yarn through the yarn on your bracelet to make a pattern or design.

As you weave and thread the yarn, recall the thread running through Scripture. Can you remember who the thread is? Show or give your bracelet to a loved one. Explain the thread and tell them about the hope we have in Jesus Christ.

Joy

Love your Life

But the angel said to them, "Don't be afraid,
for look, I proclaim to you good news of
great joy that will be for all the people:
Today in the city of David a Savior was born
for you, who is the Messiah, the Lord.

Luke 2:10-11

Following on the heels of hope, the second theme in our study of Advent is joy. For the Christian, joy can be understood as "the happy state that results from knowing and serving God."[1] It's more than mere happiness, though. The joy of the Lord is a fruit of the Spirit (Gal. 5:22) that enables a person to maintain trust and faith in Him no matter what is going on in her life (Jas. 1:2-3). As we'll see in this week's study, the joy of the Lord is wrapped up in the person and work of Jesus.

When you read the story of Jesus's birth in Scripture, you can't miss the pure joy of the people who witnessed it. Just look at a few reactions: *Mary*: "My spirit rejoices in God my Savior" (Luke 1:47). *The angel*: "I proclaim to you good news of great joy" (Luke 2:10). *The wise men*: "When they saw the star, they were overwhelmed with joy" (Matt 2:10). Being witnesses to the goodness of God and His faithfulness to keep His promises filled them with wonder and awe. The passages of Scripture we will look at this week show us that there is joy in the presence of Jesus for us, too.

DAY ONE	God promises to turn our sorrow to joy (Jer. 31:10-14)
DAY TWO	Jesus's birth is good news of great joy for all people (Luke 1–2).
DAY THREE	People find joy in the healing power of Jesus (Mark 5:21-43).
DAY FOUR	True joy is found through a connection to Jesus (John 15:1-11).
DAY FIVE	One day our joy will be complete (Rev. 19:1-10).

O COME ALL YE FAITHFUL

O come, all ye faithful,
Joyful and triumphant!
O come ye, o come ye to Bethlehem.
Come and behold him,
Born the King of angels;

O come, let us adore him;
O come, let us adore him;
O come, let us adore him,
Christ the Lord.

Sing, choirs of angels,
Sing in exultation;
Sing, all ye citizens of heav'n above
Glory to God,
All glory in the highest

Yea, Lord, we greet thee,
Born this happy morning
Jesus, to thee be all glory giv'n.
Word of the Father,
Now in flesh appearing²

WATCH THE VIDEO "Session Two: Joy" (14:21) and use the space below to take notes.

HYMN: O Come All Ye Faithful

SCRIPTURE READING: Luke 2:1-20

TO ACCESS THE VIDEO SESSIONS,
USE THE INSTRUCTIONS IN THE BACK OF YOUR BIBLE STUDY BOOK.

Discuss

If you are part of a *The Wonder of Advent* Bible study group, use this page to take notes during your group time and to keep a record of prayer requests that are mentioned.

Difference between happiness & Joy!

Happy or Sad — circumstances

Joy —

Psalm 34 V 5

Joy comes when we put our trust in the LORD!

Day 1

Let's find GOD Delightful!

FROM SORROW TO JOY
JEREMIAH 31:10-14
by Leigh Ann Dans

As a child of God, I can confidently say I've never experienced loss of any kind when I didn't also see God fill that loss with more of Himself or replace it with something better. We all remember early 2020, when the world shut down with bad news filling the airwaves of a dangerous virus. I was fearful for myself, but over and above that I was fearful for my family, especially my parents. I'm sure you can relate to what all went through my mind when the world began to lock down—what would happen to my family, my job, my health, and so on. As a single extrovert, I struggled with canceled plans and lack of contact with friends and loved ones; it was a very lonely time.

My parents asked me to come and stay with them to help, so I quarantined myself for fourteen days, and then packed up my stuff for a nine-hour drive back home. I hadn't stayed for any long periods of time with them, other than a week or two here and there, since moving to Tennessee more than thirty years ago. My busy social life came to a screeching halt, my vacation plans were canceled, my job changed from working in the office five days a week to working remote, and I was watching my church service over TV and Zoom®, from hundreds of miles away. I remember constantly thinking, "When will this be over so we can get back to normal?" Like everyone, I was grieved for my old way of life.

But in my grief and pain, God made Himself present, and He showed me that even when my plans are wrecked and everything feels uncertain, He is still good, and He is still in control.

MEMORY VERSE

My spirit rejoices in God my Savior.

Luke 1:47

Record the promise God made to His people through Jeremiah in these verses:

The Israelites had been warned by God through Jeremiah that their way of life was headed for disaster and captivity. Then just a few years later while Jeremiah was still their prophet, the first Israelites were exiled to Babylon. Can you imagine hearing the word of good news that came in Jeremiah 31? Most of what the prophet had spoken to them in the past thirty chapters of Jeremiah was not good news at all. But with the words in chapter 31, God gave them hope.

The prophet described a time when God would buy back His people and draw them back to Himself. In its immediate context this prophecy was God's promise to bring the exiles back home. But it also applies to the lengths God has gone to in order to redeem, or buy back, all people from sin.

Reminders like this one of God's goodness and power fill the pages of Scripture. As I was reading in my daily Bible study today, I came across this Scripture in 1 Samuel 16:1: "The LORD said to Samuel, 'How long are you going to mourn for Saul, since I have rejected him as king over Israel? Fill your horn with oil and go. I am sending you to Jesse of Bethlehem because I have selected for myself a king from his sons.'"

Just like I grieved the loss of my familiar and comfortable lifestyle and the world around me was in the midst of a shaking, Samuel grieved the rejection of the king of Israel, his leader. He may have been a poor king, but he was the only earthly king Samuel knew. But God didn't leave Samuel there to wallow in his despair. He told him to fill his horn with oil, and He sent him on a mission. If you know the story then you know that King David was about to arrive on the scene, the king who had a heart for God! God had a better plan for Samuel and the nation's future.

What do Jeremiah 31:10-11 and 1 Samuel 16:1 show you about the character of God?

What do these passages show you about God's work in our world and in your own life?

God always reminds us of who He is and shows us glimpses of how He is working if we are willing to look and listen.

READ JEREMIAH 31:12-14.

How would the people be changed by God's work in their lives? List everything you see in verses 12-14.

Our sorrow turned to Joy,

In these verses, we see God turning the sorrow of His people into joy. God used words like "rejoice," "goodness," "dancing," "happiness," and "satisfied" to describe His people when they returned from exile. Their joy was rooted in God's goodness (v. 14). He is their Redeemer, Comforter, Shepherd, and Provider.

We do not have to fear for the future when we know that God is good, He has plans, and His plans will prevail. As I started to try and find my new normal in a year where nothing was normal, I began to see things that God was doing in my life that would change me for the better.

For example, for years I had used the excuse that spending eight hours a day at work, then fighting traffic and being so worn out by the time I got home was why it was hard to have a consistent daily quiet time with God. But my mom, dad, and I began to take a break from our work every day and walk through the Bible together and pray. We saw (and are still seeing) answers to those daily prayers. I was able to sit daily and listen to my 83-year-old dad and my 82-year-old mom talk intimately with God. I loved them before, but God deepened my love for these two people and the faithfulness they modeled.

I've learned more about God's Word, and I've had more deep and intimate conversations with God in the past two years than I have in my entire life. Through all the instability and grief, I've fallen more deeply in love with the One who made me and redeemed me.

> Think about a time when your life circumstances changed dramatically. Name one or two ways your everyday life changed due to those circumstances.

> How do you see God's hand in those changes?

God is the same in Jeremiah's day, in the time of Jesus, and today, and so is the joy found in Him.

> READ JOHN 16:16-33.

> What did Jesus promise would bring His disciples joy?

Attitude of Gratitude

In this extended teaching from Jesus in the days leading up to His crucifixion and resurrection, Jesus told the disciples He was going away only to return. Their lives had already changed once when Jesus called them away from fishing, tax collecting, and so on, but they were about to change even more drastically. They were about to witness the event that changed the world—the death and resurrection of their leader. That moment would fill them with unimaginable sorrow.

But Jesus told them that their sorrow wouldn't last; He would turn it to joy, a joy no one would be able to take away from them. The promise of their joy was rooted in His presence with them. Not only did He not stay dead, but He also promised to be with them always through the presence of His Holy Spirit, and He promised He would one day return to wipe away every tear from the eyes of His children for good. The same Holy Spirit and the same promise of Jesus's return are ours to cling to today, and they fill us with immeasurable joy.

How does knowing that our sorrow won't last buoy your heart and mind, even in the midst of sorrowful circumstances?

Knowing there is a future.
GOD has a plan !!!

What are some practical ways you can be reminded of the joy of the Lord from day to day? How can you share that joy with others? ★

If we are satisfied with him
first — the world cannot take our
Joy away !!

Day 2

GOOD NEWS OF GREAT JOY

LUKE 1:26-56; MATTHEW 1:18-25; LUKE 2:1-20; MATTHEW 2:10

by Adrienne Camp

This week our theme for Advent is joy. As you read through the Gospels, it becomes evident that joy was the dominant emotion for everyone involved in the Christmas story when they realized what was happening at Jesus's birth (except for King Herod, of course). Our study today will look at just a few of these moments.

READ LUKE 1:26-38.

Nazareth was tiny, with only about 200-500 residents at the time of Jesus's birth.[3] We know from Scripture it didn't have the most extraordinary reputation (John 1:46). Put yourself in Mary's shoes when an angel appeared to her with a life-altering announcement: "You're going to be pregnant with the Son of God!"

> Make a list of the details Gabriel shared with Mary about God and about the child she would carry.

I wonder how many thoughts went through Mary's mind when she heard that she was favored by God (v. 28), was going to give birth to "the Son of the Most High" (v. 32), that He would be a king (v. 32), and that He would rule forever (v. 33)? Is this for real? What is Joseph going to think? How will he ever believe me? What will my parents and community think? How is any of this possible (v. 34)?

What stands out to you about Mary's two responses to Gabriel (vv. 34,38)?

Full of faith and surrendered to the Lord, even though He was demolishing any normalcy in her life and tampering with all her plans, Mary said:

> I am the Lord's servant, and I am willing to do whatever He wants. May everything you said come true.
> Luke 1:38, The Living Bible

Mary fully treasured the joy of partnering with the Lord, no matter what it could cost her—her future husband, her reputation, her body, the loss of her dreams. She took joy in knowing she was fulfilling God's will and not her own.

I can't help but wonder about the times when my dreams and plans have not gone the way I thought they should. Perhaps you've found yourself in the same place, dear sister. We can learn so much from the example Mary sets for us. Although Scripture shows us Mary's first response was one of humility and trust in the Lord and His promises, we see the fruit of that continuing in her life. She didn't just get it right the first time; her attitude of humility continued over time, and it overflowed from her heart in song.

READ LUKE 1:46-50.

Mary desired to magnify the Lord (v. 46), to make Him bigger and the central focus of her heart. Imagine taking a magnifying glass to your heart. Does each area magnify the Lord and make more of Him? I know mine certainly doesn't, although I desperately desire that it would. I pray more and more that my heart's cry would be like Mary's—filled with joy at the thought of surrendering my plans and my will to God.

Mary fully believed that God was trustworthy, even at the potential cost of what she might have to endure. Joy comes when we surrender our will to Christ. When we cast our cares on Him, we are filled with His refreshing presence. As King David wrote, "How happy is anyone who has put his trust in the Lord" (Ps. 40:4a).

What about you? Is joy a theme in your relationship with Jesus?
Explain your thoughts.

What are some of the things that limit your joy? On the other hand,
what are some times when you feel an increased joy in the Lord?

READ LUKE 2:1-18.

Write verses 10-11 in the space provided.

If you've been a Christian through even just one Christmas season, then I imagine
you're familiar with this part of the Christmas story. The angels appear to a group of
shepherds "keeping watch at night over their flock" (v. 8). Perhaps you've heard how
this scene shows us God has a heart for the down-trodden and the outcast, those who
feel as though they're on the outskirts of popular society, as shepherds were in Jesus's
day. That is true and without a doubt reflects God's heart. But that's not the only thing
going on here.

It's highly likely these were shepherds performing specific temple-related duties in
the fields of Migdal Eder, just outside of Bethlehem.[4] Their job was to search the flock
and select and protect the spotless sacrificial lambs for Passover. These shepherds
would have been well-versed in the Old Testament prophecies about the Messiah, like
these two from the prophet Micah:

> And you, watchtower for the flock, fortified hill of Daughter
> Zion, the former rule will come to you; sovereignty will come to
> Daughter Jerusalem.
> Micah 4:8

Bethlehem Ephrathah, you are small among the clans of Judah;
one will come from you to be ruler over Israel for me. His origin is
from antiquity, from ancient times.
Micah 5:2

These shepherds would have known precisely what the angelic announcement meant. The long-awaited Messiah, the rescuer of God's people, had finally been born! Imagine the relief that washed over them with this "good news of great joy" (v. 10). He's HERE! He's finally HERE! We've been waiting for so long! Joy so filled them that they became the first evangelists to tell everyone the good news of the Messiah's arrival (vv. 17-18).

When I envision myself as one of the shepherds, I can't help but wonder what my response would have been if I had heard about this promise for as long as I could remember. What would make it worth dropping everything to go investigate this news for myself? Would I be someone willing to seek the promise of Jesus in this way?

Even today, Jesus is our good news of great joy. He is our Messiah, the One who takes away the heaviness, exhaustion, and pain of life. The One who reunites us with our heavenly Father is HERE! He is Immanuel, God with us, even today (Isa. 7:14). Let the wonder and awe of what God did through the birth of Jesus fill your heart with fresh joy today.

> Take a few moments to simply sit in the presence of God today and reflect on this good news. Thank Him for always being faithful. He has never broken a promise, and He never will. ★

Day 3

ENCOUNTERING THE LIVING GOD
MARK 5:21-43; LUKE 8:40-56

by Valerie Hancock

I love a good story. Whether it's the latest blockbuster or a best-selling biography, I'm easily hooked and drawn into the events and experiences of people's lives. Stories can powerfully encourage and challenge us in ways statistics and facts can't. A person's story compels us with emotion and intrigue. We can all relate to the challenges and triumphs of others. We want to know how the story ends, but more importantly, we want to know how it unfolds.

The Bible is often described as the greatest story ever told with God as the Author, people as the characters, and Jesus Christ as the central theme. And the "greatest story" is made up of many short stories of people who have so much to teach us about the joy that comes from knowing Jesus.

While on earth Jesus met people's most pressing physical needs to give them and us a tangible picture of the healing He can bring to our lives and souls. The Gospels tell many stories of Jesus and His disciples traveling from town to town so Jesus could teach and perform miracles. Let's read one of them.

> READ MARK 5:21-43, and answer the following questions with your observations:
>
> Who are the main characters?
>
>
>
> What did each person want from Jesus?

What did Jesus say to each one?

How was each person changed by his or her interaction with Jesus?

Today's Scripture passage tells an account of two parallel stories of people who reached out to Jesus at a time of deep personal anguish and need. First was Jairus, a synagogue leader in Capernaum, who was desperate to find someone to help his dying daughter. Because synagogue leaders had close ties to the Pharisees, Jairus may have been pressured not to support Jesus. But when Jairus saw Jesus, he begged for Jesus's help. Jairus believed that if Jesus laid His hands on his daughter, she would recover—"My little daughter is dying. Come and lay your hands on her *so that she can get well and live*" (Mark 5:23, emphasis mine). So, Jesus went with him.

Along the way Jesus encountered a woman who had been dealing with a hemorrhage for twelve years. Mark points out that because of her circumstances she had suffered at the hands of physicians who were unable to heal her, and she spent all her money. What he doesn't mention but we can assume from her condition is that she was physically weak from constant blood loss, shunned in society for having a chronic disease, and ceremonially unclean and unable to worship in the presence of others at the temple. The woman's desperation was obvious.

The woman was so desperate, and her hope in Jesus's power to heal was so great, that all she wanted to do was touch His clothing in the hopes of being healed (v. 28). And she did, and she was! When the woman realized Jesus knew what had happened (vv. 30-32), she told Him everything, to which He replied "'Daughter . . . your faith has saved you. Go in peace and be healed from your affliction" (v. 34).

With verse 35, the focus shifts back to Jairus's daughter, who we now learn has died during this "interruption." Jesus went on to his house anyways. When He reached the house, He took the young girl's hand and told her to get up. And she did. "Then he took the child by the hand and said to her, 'Talitha koum' (which is translated, 'Little girl, I say to you, get up'). Immediately the girl got up and began to walk. (She was twelve years old.) At this they were utterly astounded" (Mark 5:41-42).

Can you imagine what the following days were like for the woman with the hemorrhage and Jairus's family? The retelling of what they'd seen and experienced. The profound relief of being healed. The freedom to get up and move on. The faith that was restored and strengthened. The joy that overflowed.

The Power of Faith

We all carry burdens, grief, and wounds that need healing. Some are physical. Some are spiritual. Some require miracles. They sometimes hold us back from the life God is calling us to live. At times, we desperately want the ability to get up! To carry on and go in peace! Jesus is the only One who has the life-giving power to make that a reality for us.

Both the bleeding woman and Jairus showed great faith in Jesus, believing He could change their lives just by His touch, by His presence. And they were right; He could, and He did. Do you view Jesus in the same way? Do you have faith that He can change your life? That He can heal your physical and spiritual wounds and change your circumstances?

> Write down two areas of your life that need the healing only Jesus can give. Commit them to prayer during this Advent season. Ask God to strengthen your faith, believing you can be healed.

1.

2.

The Joy of the Lord Is Your Strength

The experiences of the woman and Jairus remind us that Jesus sees us and knows our struggles. Even amid noise and confusion or when others tell us there's no hope, Jesus is there.

REREAD VERSE 34:

Daughter, your faith has saved you. Go in peace and be healed from your affliction.

Know that Jesus is speaking directly to you. That thing causing you pain may not go away, but the strength to press on through it is found in Jesus. He sees the junk we carry around that causes pain and often shame, but He wants us to live free of the burdens that hold us back or threaten to steal our joy—joy that is true and complete only in our relationship with Him.

What does verse 34 mean to you today?

Write this verse on a notecard or sticky note and post it in a place you see daily as a reminder of how Jesus's presence in your life brings hope, strength, and joy.

Jesus Is Near—Share His Joy

One of the names of God we hear often during the Christmas season is *Immanuel*, which means "God with us." God came down to dwell with us in the flesh. He "realized that power had gone out from him" (v. 30) because as God He is omniscient, the all-knowing One. No matter what you go through, you can be assured Jesus knows. He is with you in your highest highs and your lowest lows. Jesus is with you at all times and in all things. That is His promise to you. It's a promise that you can share with others this Christmas season.

Everyone needs the assurance they are not alone—even amid the countless activities of the holiday season. Maybe especially now. This is a perfect time of year to share the hope and joy you have in Christ, no matter what is happening in the world around you.

> While we wait on the second advent of Christ, how can we be the hands and feet of God to our neighbors? How can we show them God is with us every day?

I'll give you a few ideas to get you started:

- Take cookies to your neighbors (like the gingerbread cookie recipe from page 43). Attach a simple note or card sharing the joy of Christ and wishing them Merry Christmas.

- Host a pizza night for a few close friends. No fancy hors d'oeuvres or holiday attire. Ask everyone to share: What is bringing you joy this week?

- Add service men and women and local first responders and medical professionals to your Christmas card list. Let them know you're praying for them year-round.

- Volunteer at a local mission that serves people with physical needs. Pray for each person you interact with—that Jesus would be real and near to them.

- Send an email of thanks and appreciation to all your church staff and lay leaders (individually). Let them know how much you appreciate the time and commitment they put into your church's Christmas celebrations.

Advent is the season of hope, joy, peace, and love as we celebrate the birth of Christ. It is also the season we anticipate and actively wait for Christ's return. What should we do with our "in between" time? Grow in our faith. Grow in our joy. And help others to do the same. ★

Day 4

CONNECTED TO JESUS
JOHN 15:1-11

by Catherine Inman

Salty, little balloons of liquid started filling my eyes. My head became tense, and my stomach dropped. Not in a sweet, shy butterfly feeling kind of way, but in an elephant just stepped on my stomach and took all the breath out of me kind of way. I held in my hand another one-lined pregnancy test. Negative. Fast forward a few weeks, and one of my friends sends a picture of a pregnancy test with two lines to our friend group message. She's pregnant. Again. They say a picture is worth a thousand words, but I never knew it could feel like a thousand daggers.

My husband and I have been walking the infertility journey for almost three years now. It's been a season of grieving the what ifs and what could have beens. Maybe you find yourself in a season like ours, too. Maybe you didn't get that job promotion, received a negative health report, or simply never saw those dreams of yesteryear come to fruition. As we journey through life, we all have seasons of grief, confusion, and numbness. We experience difficulties that leave us with more questions than answers. Moments when happiness feels offensive, and joy is impossible to imagine. For me, I've learned those are the moments when I'm left with only one answer for how to get by—Jesus.

Joy Through Surrender

READ JOHN 15:1-11.

When Jesus spoke these words, it was part of His "Upper Room Discourse," a series of teachings Jesus gave when He was gathered with His disciples for His final Passover meal before the crucifixion. Although Jesus understood the sorrow and pain that awaited Him, His teaching abounded in joy. The Man of Sorrows (Isa. 53:3) was also the God of Joy (Ps. 16:11).

LOOK AT JOHN 15:4-5. In your own words, what does it mean to remain, or abide, in Jesus?

Joy isn't circumstantial; it's rooted in God's character. Even in the darkest of tunnels, when we can't make out a sliver of light at the end, we can trust that He's with us, and He's working. We might not always understand, but we can trust that His ways are higher than ours and His thoughts are not our thoughts (Isa. 55:8-9). Sometimes to understand, we must surrender the right to understand. We must surrender the right to have control over the situation, the right to make the plan ourselves, and the right to understand a sovereign God.

NOW READ GALATIANS 5:22-23.

When we are connected to Jesus, we bear fruit. We don't produce the fruit. We simply bear it. If we could produce the fruit on our own, there would be no need for the Vine. A branch exists for one reason, and that is to carry the fruit of the Vine.

GO BACK AND READ JOHN 15:9. What does it look like to remain in God's love? What does it *not* look like?

Joy Through Obedience

This passage also connects joy and love with obedience. Verse 10 says, "If you keep my commands you will remain in my love, just as I have kept my Father's commands and remain in his love." Jesus obeyed God, as we should long to do, too (1 John 5:3). Love and obedience go together when walking with Him. Obedience to the teachings of Jesus is a sign that we are born again believers, which allows a broken world to see the light of Christ through us. Jesus is the perfect example for us as we strive to live a life of obedience.

Look up the following Scripture passages. Next to each one, write how Jesus modeled obedience for us in that text.

Matthew 3:13-17

Matthew 4:1-11

Luke 2:51-52

John 8:21-29

Philippians 2:8

If we want to experience abundant joy, we must stay connected to the Source of joy, the true Vine—Jesus. Jesus knew that trials and afflictions would come, but He also knew that through surrender and obedience, they would be able to abide in Him and have joy to face whatever circumstance would come their way. The same is true for you and me. When our lives are rooted in Christ, all of the world's sorrows are put in perspective in light of eternity.

Looking back at the story of waiting that I shared earlier, I don't know if the Lord will choose to bless my husband and me by giving us a biological child. Some days are hopeful, while other days are filled with doubt. However, here's one thing I do know: my fulfillment, my satisfaction, and my joy will still come from Jesus alone. Why?

Because joy was never meant to be found anywhere else.

What does connection to Jesus look like for you today, or even this very hour?

Staying connected to Jesus doesn't just happen. No one accidentally connects with Jesus—at least not in any meaningful way. Hebrews 4:16 tells us that connecting to Jesus means approaching the throne of grace with boldness. It's more than going to church on Sunday. It's more than even claiming good things in His name. It's choosing Him every single day. When truly staying connected to Jesus, we can face each day with unwavering peace and genuine joy. He remains the Vine, and we, the branches. ★

Day 5

CELEBRATION IN HEAVEN
REVELATION 19:1-10
by Ravin McKelvy

Hallelujah

Have I not yearned for this day

Since the moment I first drew breath?

My God so decadently adorned in the

Praise of His creation

We, His Bride, redeemed at last

I dance in this resurrected body

My spirit is moved within me—I am home

We now see our Groom face to face

His Beauty the radiance of the sun

Hallelujah, hallelujah, hallelujah

For this feast is surely to come

Hallelujah

—Ravin McKelvy

In C. S. Lewis's *The Last Battle*, the last book in his Chronicles of Narnia series, Lewis paints a picture of new Narnia, a place where "every rock and flower and blade of grass looked as if it meant more." Upon entering this new Narnia, the Unicorn character exclaims, "I have come home at last! This is my real country! I belong here. This is the land I have been looking for all my life, though I never knew it till now."[5]

Earlier this week we looked at Jeremiah's prophecy that a day would come when God would turn the sorrow of His children to joy. Today we will look forward to Revelation 19, where we see the fulfillment of this promise and the resulting celebration. I can't help but smile as I think of the overwhelming relief this day will bring. And yet I know how easy it is to lose sight of this coming glory when we are surrounded by the realities of living in a still sinful world.

What has been on the forefront of your mind this week that has distracted you from living in light of eternity? Take a moment now to give those things over to God.

READ REVELATION 19:1-5.

List five things that stand out to you from these verses.

1.

2.

3.

4.

5.

Can you imagine the scene? Up to this point in Revelation, John has seen vision after vision of what is to come upon the return of Jesus. Now, standing before a crowd, he hears countless voices crying out together in praise and rejoicing; sin has finally been done away with!

God is just, and He will not let darkness prevail. We have never known a reality without the presence of sin, a time when grief and pain did not exist. The darkness we see before us daily can make it difficult to see the coming redemption. But these beginning verses in Revelation 19 give us a clear glimpse of what is to come: God will bring an end to every evil. This is the culmination of the story of Scripture—that God loved us so much He sent His Son to die on the cross and rise again in order for us, as disobedient people, to be with Him for eternity. And this peek into our certain future, which has huge implications for our present, is meant to give us hope. It is cause for celebration.

READ REVELATION 19:6-8 AND MATTHEW 25:1-13.

What are a few things these passages have in common?

Revelation 19:6-8 continues the vision John was given into the future events in heaven. Matthew 25:1-13 is a parable Jesus told while on earth urging His followers to be ready for His return. Both passages use imagery of a wedding feast to describe Jesus's return, with the emphasis being on preparation. Think of a newly engaged woman excited for the day she will get married. You will find her in all her spare moments preparing for the wedding—finding a dress, picking decorations, creating invitations, and on and on and on. She does all this with delight, knowing that when the day of the wedding comes, everything will be prepared for the joyous celebration.

I wonder what our lives would look like if we became more like that engaged woman, focused on the upcoming wedding feast. Think about this for a few minutes. What daily tasks would lessen in importance, and in contrast, what might we find is more urgent for daily preparation?

We may not know the date, but we know for certain that the Lord is returning for His bride. So, we must live in a constant state of preparation, keeping before us the reality of His return that we can joyously prepare. It becomes not a mundane task, but a breathtaking privilege.

On a piece of paper, write out Revelation 19:7 and stick it on your mirror or somewhere you will see it often as a daily reminder that we are preparing for the wedding feast to come.

READ REVELATION 19:9-10.

After getting a glimpse of the wedding feast, John is overwhelmed by the grandeur of it. He begins to fall down to worship the angel, but the angel rebukes him, pointing him to the only One to be worshiped—Jesus. We are reminded here, again, that this celebration is about the return of Christ and the final redemption of His Bride—you, me, His church. The angel tells John, "Worship God, because the testimony of Jesus is the spirit of prophecy."

The subject and substance of every prophecy, both in the Old and New Testaments, is the testimony of Jesus. The testimony of Jesus is the good news that He came to preach, and that good news is, indeed, that Jesus Himself is our salvation. And we who have held firmly to this testimony, truly to Christ Himself, will partake in this soul-thrilling celebration. We will at long last be home. We will be complete in the fullness of God's presence, no longer plagued by sin but rejoicing in the perfection of our Groom. We will be in the land our bodies groan to be redeemed to, that all our earthly lives our souls have ached to dwell in. Finally, we will be in our true country. That is cause for celebration today.

Daily we must live in light of the reality that God is bringing about the final destruction of sin. That we as His bride are preparing for a day that is certain to come, and in this certainty, we are given hope to face whatever today may hold.

Before you do the final exercise, take a moment to pray and ask the Lord to give you a fresh understanding of the beauty of the coming redemption so that you might live ever more fully in light of this celebration.

Having finished today's reading, write your own poem of celebration for who God is and the certainty of the redemption to come. ★

HOW TO MAKE AN EVERGREEN TABLESCAPE

by Chelsea Waack

With a variety of fresh cut evergreens and a few candles, you can transform a dining table into an inviting, aromatic space to come together with friends and family. As you work with your hands to create a beautiful tablescape, ask the Lord to fill your heart with joy for what is and what is yet to come.

SUPPLIES

- Assortment of evergreen clippings (Balsam Fir, Scotch Pine, and Leyland Cypress are a few good ones)
- Silver Dollar Eucalyptus
- Seeded Eucalyptus
- Pinecones
- Festive table runner
- 5 white pillar candles
- 8 small votive candles in glass jars
- Matches

DIRECTIONS

1. Place the table runner down the center of the table. This will help protect your table from any sap residue.

2. Arrange the evergreen clippings down the center of the table.

3. Build out the greenery, interweaving sections of eucalyptus as you go down the left and right side to create fullness.

4. Place pinecones in open spots within the greenery.

5. Alternate pillar candles on the left and right sides of the table runner. The candles should be able to sit on the runner.

6. Fill in votive candles in clusters beside the pillar candles.

7. Light candles.

8. Enjoy!

COMPLETE JOY

by Brooke Hill

Read John 15:11 together: "I have told you these things so that my joy may be in you and your joy may be complete."

Jesus doesn't just want us to have joy; He wants it to be complete. Complete means "to have all the parts." It's easy to experience joy in some of our circumstances, but it's much much more difficult to pick out the joy in the harder situations. Mary likely wasn't thrilled about giving birth far from home, but she chose to overlook that because the joy of giving birth to the Child of God greatly outweighed the less-than-perfect circumstances.

When we don't have any joy left ourselves, God has plenty: "The LORD is my strength and my shield; my heart trusts in him, and I am helped. Therefore my heart celebrates, and I give thanks to him with my song" (Ps. 28:7). What a blessing it is to rest in the strength of the Lord and the joy that is ours through Jesus.

The holiday season is filled with opportunities to make memories and reminisce about favorite times spent together. We tend to take lots of pictures to commemorate things, but we rarely print them thanks to social media's ability to preserve them instead.

This week, have your teen pick out some of his or her favorite photos from the year that's about to come to an end and print them out. Make a scrapbook or photo album full of photos that brought you joy this year. You could do your own scrapbook or just help your teen with theirs.

Include photos of times where you didn't feel the most joyful, too. Remember, Jesus desires for us to have joy in all the seasons of life. When looking back on some not-so-fun times throughout the year, discuss how you saw God's strength fill you, and what joy you could take away from the situation.

While decorating the pages, spend some time together discussing what made each of the memories so special:

- Why did they bring you joy?

- How can you be intentional about creating that joy again?

- How can you be intentional about sharing that joy with others?

This is a great, tangible way to be reminded of God's faithfulness throughout the year.

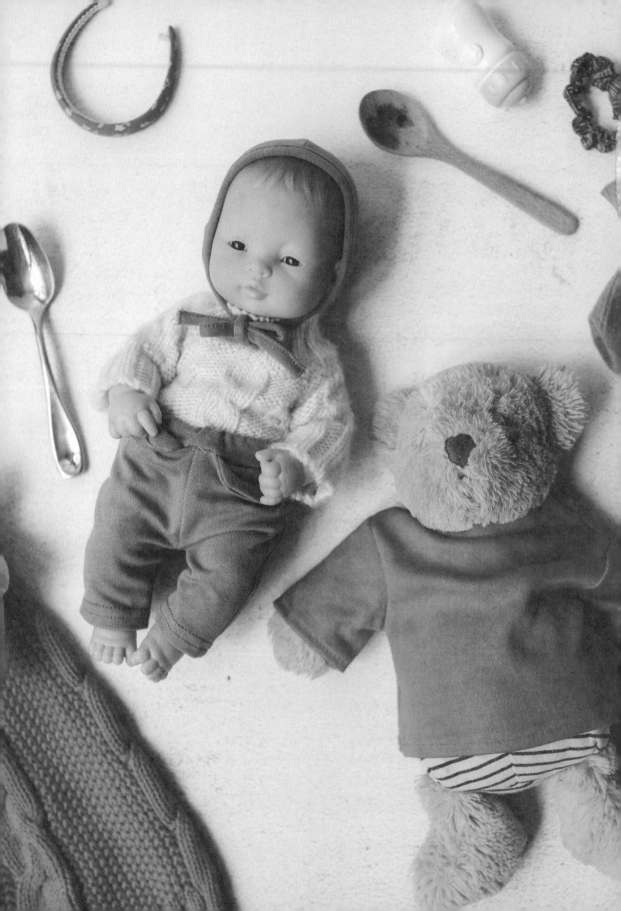

LITTLE BLESSINGS

by Bekah Stoneking

Form teams and gather a baby doll for each team. If you don't have dolls, you can play this game with stuffed animals, instead.

Challenge each team to race through your home on a scavenger hunt, searching for creative items to use to "dress" your babies. Each baby needs something for a diaper, an outfit, a cozy hat, a bottle, and a toy. The team that gathers all five items and dresses their baby first, wins.

After the game, take a few minutes to talk through these questions:

Who was the most creative?

Which baby item was the funniest?

How did you feel during the game?

You might have felt excited and nervous during the scavenger hunt. The people in the Christmas story probably felt similar emotions as they anticipated Jesus's arrival. But they also felt another emotion—joy!

The Bible tells us that Elizabeth, Mary, the shepherds, and the wise men were all full of joy because of Jesus's birth. Seeing God keep His promise to send the Messiah filled them with joy, wonder, and awe.

Jesus continued to bring people joy throughout His time on the earth. During His ministry Jesus met needs, healed people, and performed miracles. People were joyful in His presence.

You can learn to live like Jesus and experience joy in Jesus's presence, too, when you help meet people's needs. One way to do this is by helping families welcome their new babies home.

Work with your family to make a list of things babies need. Which item on the list do you think is most important? Go shopping for that item or for various supplies needed for feeding, bathing, diapering, or dressing babies, then deliver the items to your church or to another ministry in your area that supports pregnant women.

PRAY

Pray for parents and for their babies. Thank God for creating these children and for the blessing of their lives.

Peace

"Peace I leave with you. My peace I give to you.
I do not give to you as the world gives. Don't
let your heart be troubled or fearful."

John 14:27

Discord and conflict are everywhere. When we look at the culture we live
in, it's hard to imagine the peace God promises to our world being possible.
Our present reality is one of the reasons we know God's work isn't done,
and it's good motivation for us to eagerly anticipate Jesus's return.

Through His first Advent, Jesus made peace between God and His children
possible. This peace is available to all who believe in Jesus and experience
the work of the Holy Spirit in our lives. But God also promises a day when
peace—both human-to-God and human-to-human will be the universal
reality forever. That is the day we long for.

In the meantime, the passages we'll study this week will help us understand
how Jesus helps us navigate a chaotic world with a peace that passes
understanding (Phil. 4:7).

DAY ONE	God promises to restore peace to His creation (Ezek. 34).
DAY TWO	Jesus's birth revealed Him to be God's instrument of peace (Luke 2:22-40).
DAY THREE	The forgiveness and freedom of Jesus brings peace to fearful hearts (John 8:1-11).
DAY FOUR	Jesus teaches about His ministry of peace (John 14:27-31).
DAY FIVE	Everlasting peace awaits us (Rev. 19:11–20:15).

O
COME
EMMANUEL

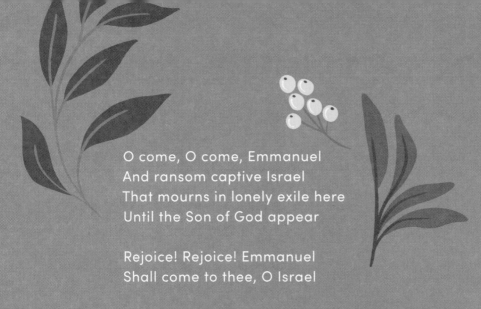

O come, O come, Emmanuel
And ransom captive Israel
That mourns in lonely exile here
Until the Son of God appear

Rejoice! Rejoice! Emmanuel
Shall come to thee, O Israel

O come, Thou Dayspring, come and cheer
Our spirits by Thine advent here
Disperse the gloomy clouds of night
And death's dark shadows put to flight

Rejoice! Rejoice! Emmanuel
Shall come to thee, O Israel

O come, Thou Wisdom from on high
And order all things, far and nigh
To us the path of knowledge show
And cause us in her ways to go

Rejoice! Rejoice! Emmanuel
Shall come to thee, O Israel

O come, desire of nations, bind
In one the hearts of all mankind
Bid Thou our sad divisions cease
And be Thyself our King of peace

WATCH THE VIDEO "Session Three: Peace" (12:43) and use the space below to take notes.

HYMN: O Come, O Come Emmanuel

SCRIPTURE READING: Luke 2:25-38

TO ACCESS THE VIDEO SESSIONS,
USE THE INSTRUCTIONS IN THE BACK OF YOUR BIBLE STUDY BOOK.

Discuss

If you are part of a *The Wonder of Advent* Bible study group, use this page to take notes during your group time and to keep a record of prayer requests that are mentioned.

Day 1

EVERLASTING PEACE
EZEKIEL 34:1-31

by Tina Boesch

When I woke up this morning, I pulled the curtains aside and discovered there was a dusting of snow covering the shrubs, lawns, and rooftops. The dark ash color of the bare oak and maple branches outside my window stood in sharp contrast to the light reflecting off the freshly fallen snow.

The barrenness of winter can feel like exile from the conditions of spring. Spring is the season of growth when rain, sunlight, and warmth combine to create conditions amenable to the flourishing of plants, fruit trees, and flowers. But during the abbreviated chill days of winter, nothing grows. It's as if the earth is dormant and waiting—waiting for the sustained warmth of the sun and the blessing of spring rains.

The "exile" of winter is endurable because we know the conditions don't last. Spring inevitably arrives cloaked in daffodils and azalea blossoms. But when the nation of Israel was exiled in Babylon, the people often lost sight of the hope of an end to their winter of suffering. They had experienced the brutality of war, the destruction of Jerusalem, captivity in a foreign land—all consequences of their own sin, disobedience, and idolatry. Far from home, far from peace, despairing and disillusioned, they forgot the promises of God, His faithfulness in the past, and His present mercies. And so, God inspired prophets like Ezekiel to speak hope into the pain of exile.

Let's look for signs of spring in Ezekiel 34, a prophecy written for God's people while they were exiled in Babylon.

READ EZEKIEL 34:1-21. In the columns below record words from the passage that describe the shepherds of Israel and words that describe how God will shepherd His people.

SHEPHERDS OF ISRAEL	GOD AS SHEPHERD

Looking at the descriptions you've written above, what do you think is the most meaningful difference between God and the shepherds of Israel?

What a stark contrast! Not only had the leaders of Israel been indifferent to the suffering of the people; they had even been taking advantage of them. But God saw. God cared. And God promised that He would rescue and gather His scattered people. An attentive shepherd always seeks and saves His lost sheep.

NOW READ EZEKIEL 34:22-24.

What is the central promise of verse 23?

This prophecy was written hundreds of years after the reign of King David. Remember that when David was a young shepherd, God chose him and anointed him as king. David was also a musician, and he penned Psalm 23, the beloved meditation on the Lord as our shepherd who guides, protects, and restores our souls. Ezekiel 34:23 isn't promising that David will be resurrected to once more shepherd Israel; it's promising that God will send a Messiah—a shepherd in the line of King David—to care for His people and lead them to freedom.

TURN TO JOHN 10:11-17 AND READ JESUS'S WORDS.

Compare the description of God as a shepherd from Ezekiel 34 with
what Jesus says of Himself in John 10. Write down a few of
your observations.

What else does Jesus say He will do as the Good Shepherd?
(See verses 15 and 17.)

Jesus fulfilled Ezekiel's prophecy that there would be "one shepherd" (Ezek. 34:23)
to lead God's flock. In addition to tending the sheep, Jesus would lay down His life
for them. Jesus's sacrificial death—a death born of God's great love for His people
(John 3:16)—would facilitate the peace that Ezekiel foresaw but that the people hadn't
yet experienced.

READ EZEKIEL 34:25-31.

LOOK AT VERSE 25. Who made the covenant, and what sort of
covenant would it be?

A covenant is a formal, binding agreement. God Himself drafted, signed, and enacted
the "covenant of peace." This covenant would be different in some important ways
from the covenant made with Moses and the Israelites at Mount Sinai after the exodus
(Ex. 19–24), a covenant the people of Israel proved incapable of obeying.

TURN TO JEREMIAH AND READ 31:31-34.

The "new covenant" Jeremiah describes is the same as the "covenant of peace" promised in Ezekiel 34. List at least two things you learned about this covenant from Jeremiah.

God's "covenant of peace" is centered in His grace and assures us that He plans to redeem and restore people broken by sin. At the heart of this covenant were God's promises to write His law on their hearts and to forgive their sins forever. The peace promised is so much more than the absence of conflict. This is the peace of shalom, the peace of restored relationships, security, well-being, and flourishing communities living within a blessed, healthy, renewed environment.[2]

LOOK AGAIN AT EZEKIEL 34:25-31.

Can you think of a time when you've experienced this sort of peace in your own life? If so, describe that experience. If not, why do you think that may be?

I long for the kind of existence Ezekiel describes in this passage, and I bet you do too. How could we not? All of us want to live in a world free from external threats and internal fears. Some of the threats mentioned in this passage may feel foreign to those of us living in the modern world—not many of us have dangerous wild creatures lurking in the shadows around our homes. And for many of us, our stocked fridges and pantries ensure we don't fret about famine. But we can empathize with those living in the ancient world for whom these threats were very real and with many of our neighbors who still struggle with food insecurity. Although today we're not likely to be prey for lions and panthers, the beasts of cancer, Alzheimer's, drug addiction, anxiety, and depression may be stalking us or those we love. Ezekiel's prophecy assures us that God doesn't intend for us to live in a constant state of fear. Instead, we were created to live securely in God's presence.

> Spend a moment considering areas in your life in which you most long to experience God's peace. Pray for God's peace to be realized in those areas or relationships where you most feel it lacking.

All those who know Jesus as Messiah and Lord have entered into the covenant of peace with God through the blood of Christ. But even though Jesus's work of redemption on the cross is complete, creation waits for the full restoration we glimpse in Ezekiel 34—an all-embracing, healing, enduring peace. During Advent, we anticipate the day this peace will be fully realized when Christ returns to make all things new. And as people who follow the Prince of Peace, we carry the gospel of peace into the weary world. Notice that in verse 26 God promises, "I will make [my people] and the area around my hill a blessing." You were created to become a blessing. You were designed to be an instrument of God's peace!

> Reflect on how you might be able to extend the peace of the Lord today. How could you be a blessing to a friend, neighbor, or family member? ★

Day 2

GOD'S INSTRUMENT OF PEACE
LUKE 2:21-40
by Elizabeth Hyndman

When I was growing up, there was a woman at our church known to everyone as "Miss Frances." She came to church every time it was open, her hair in a neat gray bun. She rocked babies in the nursery and taught preschoolers about missions. She smiled as elementary school kids raced past her, despite several "Do not run!" attempts from their parents.

Miss Frances was a faithful church member who sang in the choir, attended Sunday School, and served in every way she could. She was a widow, and her children did not live close by, but the church stepped in when she needed a ride or extra help. She was a devoted member of our church family, and I think of her when I hear the story of Simeon and Anna in Luke 2.

READ LUKE 2:21-24.

Why did Mary, Joseph, and Jesus come to Jerusalem?

Why do you think it was important for Mary and Joseph to follow the law in this way?

Mary and Joseph had already shown themselves to be obedient to God, and Jesus's circumcision and presentation at the temple was another example of that obedience. Jesus was the firstborn in His earthly family and the one and only Son of God, the firstborn of all creation (Col. 1:15). The law for the dedication of the firstborn mentioned in Luke 2:23 was given after the Passover in Egypt. This ceremony and redemption of the firstborn son was to serve as a reminder of God's rescue of His people and to dedicate the firstborn into God's service.³ The Israelites could point to this ritual and say, See what God has done for us (Ex. 13:11-16). This early moment in Jesus's life on earth points to His purpose. He is redeemed as the firstborn, and He will redeem us with His life.

READ LUKE 2:25-35.

Everything we know about Simeon is contained in these verses. I love how one commentary frames it: "Who he was was unimportant for Luke. Only the role he played in Jesus's story is important."⁴

We know that Simeon was a righteous man, and the Holy Spirit was on him. He was looking forward to the day when God's plan for His people would be fulfilled in the Messiah. He went to the temple on this particular day under the guidance of the Holy Spirit.

Does anything about Simeon's prayer surprise you? What about his words to Mary? Explain.

In verse 32, Simeon claimed that the salvation he saw with the coming of this Christ child would be a "light for revelation to the Gentiles and glory to your people Israel." The Old Testament reveals that Israel already had divine revelation; God made Himself known to them through His words and His work. But Jesus, the Messiah, came to reveal God's salvation as available for all people.

At Christmastime, we often talk about Jesus as the Prince of Peace. And it is true— Jesus died and rose again so that we might have peace with God. Romans 4:25–5:1 says, "He was delivered up for our trespasses and raised for our justification. Therefore, since we have been justified by faith, we have peace with God through our Lord Jesus Christ." However, when Simeon spoke to Mary, he told her that Jesus's ministry would not be without conflict.

READ MATTHEW 10:32-39. How does this passage reflect what Simeon predicted for Mary in Luke 2?

Why do you think Jesus (in Matthew 10) and Simeon (in Luke 2) spoke of Jesus bringing conflict?

In thinking through the passage in Matthew, Aaron Wilson wrote, "As much as the gospel brings peace between God and sinners, it also brings division between those aligned with Jesus and those who reject Him."[5] And this is the conflict Simeon predicted as well. "The fall and rise of many" shows how people will react differently to the message of Christ—some will choose to follow Jesus, while others will reject Him. Eventually, that conflict led to Jesus's death—a sword that pierced His mother's soul.

What about you? Have you ever experienced conflict with others because of your faith in Christ?

READ LUKE 2:36-38. Here we meet Anna. What do we know about Anna from this passage?

Like Simeon, this is Anna's only appearance in Scripture. Why do you think Luke included this story and these details about Anna's life?

Anna was a steadfast servant of the Lord. The details that she was a prophetess and basically at church every time the doors were opened (like Miss Frances) lent her credibility to Luke's audience. This woman was devout. And she, too, confirmed that Jesus was the One who came to redeem God's people.

READ LUKE 2:39-40.

We close out Jesus's family's time at the temple with a note that Mary and Joseph had "completed everything according to the law of the Lord." Mary and Joseph were pious parents raising Jesus according to the law God had given to His people for their good and His glory.

Finally, we read that Jesus "grew up and became strong, filled with wisdom, and God's grace was on him." This reflects what was also said about John the Baptist in Luke 1:80.

READ LUKE 1:80 AND COMPARE IT WITH LUKE 2:40. What was added to Jesus's description that was not in John's?

What does that teach us about Jesus and His mission?

I love that this part of Jesus's life is included in Scripture. This story gives us a glimpse of faithful believers—parents prioritizing God's Word, saints following the leading of the Spirit, and the faithfulness of a prophetess to be in the right place to meet the Messiah. We're also reminded of the purpose of this boy's life. Jesus was sent from the Father, full of divine wisdom and grace, in order to save us from our sins and restore peace to our relationship with our heavenly Father. Jesus's mission was clear from the beginning of His time on earth.

Going to church, serving, reading Scripture, praying, even the day-to-day tasks of showing up for work or raising children, can sometimes feel tedious or like they don't really matter. In this story, we see that all those things are not for naught. God sent His Son to meet us in the every day. For our part, we remain devoted. We do not grow "tired of doing good" (Gal. 6:9).

Do you know someone like Anna or Simeon—a faithful servant, perhaps behind the scenes, whose life is dedicated to serving God?

Write that person's name here: _____ Say a prayer of thanks to God for that person's faithfulness in pointing others to Him. Consider sending that person a note or a quick text of encouragement today. ★

Day 3

WORDS OF LIFE
JOHN 8:1-11
by Erin Franklin

Words are powerful. They can encourage, convict, or demoralize. Words paired with action are the most powerful. I'm sure you can think back to a time when a parent, teacher, or coach said something that you remember to this day.

> Write down an example of a word of wisdom an authority figure spoke to you that you still remember.

In John 1:1, Jesus is described as "the Word," demonstrating the power and eternality of the Word of God. Rabbi Abraham Joshua Heschel once said, "Speech has power and few men realize that words do not fade. What starts out as a sound ends in a deed."[6] Throughout the Gospels, we see Jesus use words to both forgive and convict. In our Scripture passage today, He speaks life-giving peace into a woman's life—the same peace He offers to you and me today.

> READ JOHN 8:1-11.

> What are some questions you have after reading this passage?

You may notice in your Bible that before John 7:53 it says something like, "[The earliest mss do not include 7:53–8:11.]" Scholars question if this passage, sometimes referred to as the "Pericope Adulterae," was originally part of John's Gospel since it doesn't appear in the earliest manuscripts. Some commentators believe it may have been added later, perhaps because it was an oral account that scribes later added to preserve the tradition. Others believe it was removed from the older manuscripts because religious leaders thought Jesus to be too lenient with the woman and her sin.[7] Whatever the case, we know this story accurately fits with Jesus's teaching and His character, and we can believe the truth it communicates.

While Jesus was teaching in the temple, the scribes and Pharisees (religious leaders) brought a woman caught in adultery to Him. Verse 6 tells us their goal was to "test" or "trap" Jesus: "They asked this to *trap* him, in order that they might have evidence to accuse him" (emphasis added). The test was this: if Jesus said not to stone the woman, He would be breaking Jewish law (Deut. 22:22). If He said to stone her, He would be breaking Roman law, which prohibited Jews from carrying out capital punishment. (See John 18:31.) It seems the primary intention of the Pharisees was to undermine Jesus's authority rather than to make sure the law was being upheld.

> READ DEUTERONOMY 22:22, the law the religious leaders mentioned in John 8:5. Who must die, according to this verse? What insight does this give you into the religious leaders' intentions in John 8?

According to the law of Moses from Deuteronomy 22, both the man and the woman caught in adultery must die as punishment for their sin. So, where is the man the woman was with in this story? John 8:4 says the woman was "caught in the act," but the leaders failed to bring the man to Jesus. It's clear the leaders were not concerned about justice; rather, they wanted to build their case against Jesus.

> REREAD JOHN 8:6-9. Then use the space below to summarize Jesus's words from verse 7 in your own words.

Jesus acknowledged that the woman was a sinner. She was guilty, no question. But so were those who sought to sentence her. Paul reminds us, "all have sinned and fall short of the glory of God" (Rom. 3:23). Jesus's statement reminded the leaders that they were sinners too.

We don't know what Jesus wrote in the dust, but several scholars have presented ideas. Perhaps Jesus wrote the sins of the religious leaders, or perhaps He wrote their names (or the names of others they sinned with). The content is not revealed, only the convicting power of His writing. Whatever He wrote, the message clearly made an impact on those around Him. After they all left one by one, only Jesus remained with the sinful woman because only Jesus had the authority to cast the first stone. But the foundation of Jesus's ministry is mercy and grace, so He offered her an opportunity to repent instead of delivering the punishment she deserved according to the strict interpretation of Jewish law.

REREAD VERSES 10-11. What is the significance of Jesus's question to the adulteress in verse 10?

Did Jesus condone her sin?

NOW, TURN TO JOHN 5 AND READ VERSES 1-16. How is Jesus's command in John 5:14 similar to His instruction in John 8:11?

What do you learn about Jesus and His ministry from these two interactions?

Jesus didn't condone the adulteress's sin in John 8; He told her to stop her sinful behavior. Based on the law, the woman deserved death, but He offered her freedom and forgiveness. He offered her life, and He brought peace to her fearful heart because she no longer had to live in a state of rejection, fear, and turmoil. The same is true for the man in 5:14.

John Piper notes that Jesus's message is not "'neither do I condemn you, so it doesn't matter if you commit adultery.' Instead, His message is 'I am reestablishing righteousness in your life . . . Don't commit adultery anymore. Not mainly because you fear stoning. But because you have met God, and have been rescued by his grace — saved by grace!'"[8] We don't know if the woman heeded Jesus's instruction to sin no more, but we can be assured that Jesus came not to condemn us, but to save us, offering opportunity for us to repent and turn from our sin.

> "For God did not send his Son into the world to condemn the
> world, but to save the world through him."
> John 3:17

Our longing for forgiveness should not primarily be because we want to avoid condemnation but because we desire the perfect righteousness found only through Jesus. The peace Jesus brought to this woman's soul is the same He offers to everyone who will repent of their sins and believe in Him. His words of mercy—"Neither do I condemn you"—stand the test of time, offering hope to generations of sinners.

How does reading Jesus's words in today's passage bring you peace? Take a few minutes to reflect on the truths you learned from studying God's Word today. ★

Day 4

MY PEACE I GIVE YOU
JOHN 14:27-31

by Kim Massey

Today we continue in our Advent study through the theme of peace. Last week was powerful as we reflected on the wondrous theme of joy, which is so fitting to talk about before we consider God's promise of peace.

Growing up, part of the nightly prayer my mom led us in (which I still say to this day!) is asking our God for "joy through everything and peace beyond my understanding." My mom was a homemaker and mother of three young girls when she became a widow. My father passed away unexpectedly when I was very young, and a month later my mom lost her younger brother and only sister one day apart from each other. Through that grief, I watched God give my mom the peace she needed to get through every day, and I felt His peace, too.

God gave my mother the strength to push us in ways that a mother and father must do, the strength to not put her limitations on us, and the strength to tell us and show us that when we hit hard times it is only a sign that we must lean in stronger to our faith. The thing that makes my mother's story of peace and her entire journey with Christ remarkable to me is that she made the daily decision to trust God and have peace instead of letting her situation get the best of her.

My mother didn't have it easy in life by any means. She never had anyone to speak life into her. None of her family visited her when she was in college, even though she was the first and only of her siblings to attend. I don't think it's because they didn't love her; I think her world was foreign to them and they didn't understand the magnitude of her accomplishment or what visits from them would mean to her. But it was devastating to my mom to feel like she didn't have the support of her family during such a monumental time in her life. She worked several jobs throughout college and had to start and stop many times before finishing her degree 20 years down the line. However, in all of this, she made the choice to believe God's promises and to live at peace with her family, with her journey, and with her losses. My mother to this day is so full of joy you would think she always had a life of roses.

You may not be able to relate to my mom's struggles, but I know you have your own. In the Bible passage we will look at today, Jesus says, "Peace I leave with you. My peace I give to you. I do not give to you as the world gives. Don't let your heart be troubled or fearful" (John 14:27). There's so much to trouble us in this world, but it gives me such joy to know that the only thing we have to do for peace is to believe in Jesus.

Let's look more closely at Jesus's encouraging words and see what good news there is for us.

READ JOHN 14:27-31.

Glance back at John 13:1, which gives some helpful context for chapter 14. What did Jesus know at that point in time that His disciples didn't?

Jesus's teaching in John 14 is one of my favorite passages in the Bible. In this scene, Jesus and His disciples are gathered around a table to celebrate the Passover meal, and Jesus knows it is His last meal with His followers before the crucifixion. They don't realize this of course, but that looming event is at the forefront of Jesus's mind as He encourages His disciples with His promise of peace.

In verse 27, Jesus says the peace we find in Him is different from the peace we find from the things of the world. List anything you can think of that a person might turn to for peace. What do you tend to turn to in search of peace?

In your own words, how is the peace Jesus offers different from the world's? Think back to what you've learned from the first three days of study this week to help you answer.

The peace of Christ stands in direct contrast to the unrest of our world and the anxieties in our hearts, and it is a defining characteristic of Jesus's mission. God didn't create a world full of chaos and conflict. That is an aspect of our sinful, broken world. He also never wanted us to search out wholeness and fulfillment from things like human relationships, shopping, social media, work identity, or any other worldly goods or relationships. All of those things are fine, but they can't offer us the rest we're meant to find in God. My mom never would have found the peace she found through her grief anywhere other than from Jesus.

> READ JOHN 14:28-29 AGAIN. Imagine you were one of Jesus's disciples who had surrendered your life to following Him and participating in His ministry. What might you have been thinking and feeling as you listened to these words?

Jesus's call for peace in His absence is one that I imagine His disciples did not want to hear. I think about it like this: If I have Jesus here, right in front of me, showing me how to live and teaching me about life in the kingdom of God, of course I would be very upset at the thought of Him leaving! The disciples didn't have the complete picture we have. They didn't know Jesus's time on earth was only the beginning of the story.

Jesus knew He would have to die, that He would be raised from the dead, and that He would go to dwell in heaven with the Father until the time for His second advent. Because He came to earth to die for our sins on the cross and because He defeated death when He rose from the grave, He restored our relationship with the Father. While His earthly ministry was nearing the end, He promised His disciples a Counselor—the Holy Spirit—who would be with them and remind them of all He taught them. This is why we rejoice and give praise for Jesus's first advent.

Because humans are skeptical by nature, Jesus made it a point to clearly predict His own death to His disciples so that their faith in Him didn't waiver when that time came (v. 29). What does this mean for us? No matter what we are going through, when things don't go how we planned or imagined they would, we have a Savior who is never surprised by the chaos of our world. He has a plan.

REREAD JOHN 14:30-31. Who is the ruler of the world Jesus mentions here? (For help, look at John 12:30-31.)

What does Jesus say about him?

How does knowing this truth strengthen you during your own times of sorrow or suffering?

In verse 30, Jesus says, "I will not talk with you much longer, because the ruler of the world is coming. He has no power over me." The ruler of the world is Satan, and what a reminder for us that he has zero power over God. The next days of Jesus's life would make it seem like Satan gained control, but Jesus reminds us that He was actually following the commands of God (v. 31). I have peace in knowing that of all the attacks Satan makes on my life, the lives of loved ones, and the things I hear about in the world around me, he will never succeed if my life is rooted in Christ. In today's world, with so much information at our disposal, even misinformation from people who mean well, it is all the more important to be rooted in Christ. We are all human, and no one on earth is perfect. Because of this, we are to love everyone as Christ loves us and to put our trust in our heavenly Father, knowing that eternal life is promised.

I'll leave you with Isaiah 53:5.

> But he was pierced because of our rebellion, crushed because of our iniquities; punishment for our peace was on him, and we are healed by his wounds.

Sister, you and I are healed by Jesus's wounds. His punishment brought our peace, our restored relationship with God. The peace that only He can give us is not only within reach, it is already in us through the power of the Holy Spirit. May God be with you as you choose Him daily, receive the peace only He can give you, and encourage others to do the same. ★

Day 5

PEACE WILL PREVAIL
REVELATION 19:11–20:15

by Debbie Dickerson

The summer after I turned 12, I spent hours sitting high in a tree. The sturdy arms of the oak leaned low for me to hoist myself up to a ready-made pew in the arch of a branch, where I'd retreat from the gravity of grief left by my granddaddy's death. There in the shaded sun, I'd fix my gaze upward with thoughts of my granddaddy in heaven, and in God's presence I felt His peace.

It is true, as Elisabeth Elliot said, "Suffering is never for nothing."[9] That unrest within us and the chaos around us create a longing to be in the presence of God, where finally we find peace.

> What is drawing you to God today? The pain of loss? Conflict in a relationship? Fear of chaos? Before we study a glorious time when peace will prevail, talk with God about your trials. Ask for His peace today.

READ REVELATION 19:11-16.

Jesus came as a baby to Bethlehem to make peace between God and us. This passage describes Jesus's second coming when He'll establish peace between others and us and throughout all creation.

Compare what happened when Jesus first came with the promise of what will happen when He comes again. Fill in the chart with what you observe.

He came as a baby in a manger (Luke 2:7).	Read Revelation 19:11.
An angel announced His birth to shepherds (Luke 2:11).	Read Matthew 24:29-31.
He was wrapped in cloth (Luke 2:7).	Read Revelation 19:13.
He was named Jesus (Matt. 1:18-21).	Read Revelation 19:11-13,16 and Isaiah 9:6.
A crown of thorns was placed on His head (Matt. 27:29).	Read Revelation 19:12.
Soldiers mockingly called Him king of the Jews (Matt. 27:29).	Read Revelation 19:16 and Philippians 2:10-11.

Jesus once rode a donkey on His way to the cross. But in visions of the future, we're given a taste of His glorious return. Suddenly, the sun darkens, and the heavens shake with the parting sky (Matt. 24:29). There He is, mounted on a white horse: the Faithful and True Rider, crowned victorious. This is the moment our hearts have been longing for!

The blood on His robe reminds us of the wounds He suffered on the cross for our sins. But as one commentator points out, these stains also remind us of the many foes He has defeated throughout all redemptive history—the same foes we fought before surrendering them to Him. (See Isa. 63:1-6.)[10] Perhaps you recognize some of your own foes, ways the enemy has wounded you with grief, strife, or anxiety.

List some of the "foes" Jesus has defeated for you.

READ PHILIPPIANS 3:7-11. When you look at today's troubles through the lens of Paul's words in Philippians and the future promise of Revelation 19, what are your biggest takeaways?

READ REVELATION 19:17–20:3. What happens to the beast and the false prophet?

What do the monikers of Satan in Revelation 20:2 reveal about him? What happens to Satan?

Although we get a picture of Jesus's return from Revelation, much remains a mystery to us, including the timeline of these events. Because prophecy contains both symbolic and literal descriptions, Christians differ in their interpretation of how these future promises will play out, and that's OK. The main focus is that God has made clear the blessings that await believers and the warning for unbelievers at the return of Jesus.

Regardless of when it happens and exactly how, we can be assured that Jesus, our beloved Savior, will triumph over evil. The song "Joy to the World" belongs here! We sing it at Christmas, but at Christ's second coming, the words will be our reality. With evil erased, we'll celebrate: "No more let sins and sorrows grow, nor thorns infest the ground. He comes to make his blessings flow far as the curse is found."[11]

Look around. What are some things you're relieved to know will be no more?

READ REVELATION 20:4-6.

Whom do you see? What will they do? Imagine yourself among the glorified saints!

Since the fall in the garden, God has been preparing His children for the day when He will restore our broken world. God will fulfill His promise to restore the goodness of the garden of Eden. God will keep the covenant of peace we studied in Ezekiel 34. Trees will yield fruit, the wolf will lodge with the lamb, the lame will leap, and hearts will be holy. "Then they will know that I, the LORD their God, am with them" (Ezek. 34:30).

> Select two passages below. Write out key words and phrases from those verses that help you create a collage of words depicting this time of glorious peace:
>
> • Isaiah 9:6-7
>
> • Isaiah 11:6-9
>
> • Isaiah 35:1-8
>
> • Daniel 7:27

Christ's kingdom is coming, and He is using chaos and conflict to equip us to reign with Him. (See Jas. 1:1-12.) When we view our trials as a training ground, we can celebrate that "our momentary light affliction is producing for us an absolutely incomparable eternal weight of glory" (2 Cor. 4:17).

> Ask God to give you a glimpse of how He is preparing you through your trials for His glory.

READ REVELATION 20:7-15.

A last sobering scene we can't miss is the picture of Satan's final moments. We may wonder why Satan is released to deceive the nations, but God shows us once more His justice in judging those who rebel against Him, even in a perfect world.

> What does this passage reveal about the human heart?

Conflict and chaos reflect deeply rooted sin in this fallen world. Why are we utterly dependent on God for salvation? (See p. 167 for an explanation of God's plan of salvation.)

In a futile attempt, Satan gathers his innumerable army for battle, only to be consumed by fire falling from heaven. Satan is cast into the lake of fire, and "the dead, the great and the small" (v. 12) are summoned before the great white throne. From the book of life and the books recording their deeds, Jesus judges them. All unbelievers are sentenced to indescribable and unending punishment. But those who have trusted in Jesus as their Savior will never face condemnation. (See Rom. 8:1-2; 1 Cor. 3:14-15; and Eph. 2:8-10.) Hallelujah! What a Savior!

How does the grace and forgiveness you've received from Jesus compel you to share the hope you've found in Him?

What a different perspective God gives us when we come and rest in His presence. His Spirit fills us with peace as He draws us closer to Him and equips us to serve Him. As you celebrate Jesus's first coming, envision His second coming and see your life in light of that time when peace will prevail. ★

HOW TO MAKE CHRISTMAS SPICE TEA

by Chelsea Waack

Stay warm and cozy by the fire with a cup of Christmas Spice Tea. Treasure the good news of Jesus's birth in your heart as you take the first sip. Let this be a small representation of peace on earth—beginning with peace in your home.

SUPPLIES

- 26 oz pineapple juice
- 1 can frozen concentrate orange juice
- 6 oz fresh lemon juice
- 2 cups of sugar
- 4 1/2 quarts of water
- 4 cinnamon sticks
- 1 tablespoon of cloves
- 6 Constant Comment® tea bags
- Mini candy canes

DIRECTIONS

1. Heat pineapple juice, orange juice concentrate, lemon juice, sugar, and 4 quarts of water in a large pan until sugar is dissolved.

2. In a separate pan, add 2 cups of water, cinnamon sticks, cloves, and tea bags. Bring to a boil and simmer for 10 minutes.

3. Combine both pans of ingredients. Serve hot in a small mug with a candy cane.

TIP

To keep the tea warm for the entire evening, pour into an electric hot beverage dispenser.

PEACE AND QUIET

by Brooke Hill

Read Philippians 4:7 together: "The peace of God, which surpasses all understanding, will guard your hearts and minds in Christ Jesus." For me, this verse is one of the ways that I just know, deep in my soul, that God is real.

One of the most peaceful things I enjoy is a nice warm bubble bath. I don't treat myself to the extra fun bath bombs and body care treats often, so when I do, it's extra special. Here are some instructions for making a Peppermint Bath Bomb to make with your teen. It's a nice, Christmas-scented, relaxing treat that you can make for yourselves or plan to gift to sisters, aunts, grandmothers, or friends.

SUPPLIES

- 1 cup baking soda
- 1/2 cup epsom salts
- 1/2 cup citric acid
- 3 teaspoons apricot oil
- 2 teaspoons peppermint essential oil
- water in a spray bottle
- Mold of your choice (snowflake, Christmas tree, a circle, whatever you choose)

DIRECTIONS

1. Mix all dry ingredients in a bowl.

2. Mix the apricot oil and the peppermint essential oil in a container you can easily pour from.

3. Slowly add the oils to the dry ingredients. Mix thoroughly.

4. Spray water slowly in the dry ingredients, mixing well after every spray. (Adding the water too quickly will make it fizz prematurely.)

5. The mixture should feel kind of like damp sand, and it should be able to hold its shape. Next, press the mixture into your mold and let dry at least overnight, and possibly for up to 24 hours depending on the size.

6. Store in an airtight container.[11]

JESUS BRINGS PEACE

by Bekah Stoneking

Two things are opposites when they are completely different from each other. When Jesus lived on the earth, there was conflict, sadness, and fear everywhere. King Herod's reign was cruel and chaotic. People were breaking their promises to each other. Even the disciples felt worry and confusion. But Jesus offered something completely different. Jesus offered the opposite. Jesus offered peace.

Isaiah 9 named the Messiah the Prince of Peace and all throughout the New Testament, Jesus told His followers to not fear but to be at peace instead.

Sin, conflict, sadness, and fear still exist in our world today. But because of Jesus, we can have peace and we can be reconciled to God.

GAME
Play a game of opposites with your family members. Work as individuals or on teams to see who can name the most pairs of opposites in three minutes. We've listed a few in the next column to get you started.

- What is the opposite of up?
- What is the opposite of hot?
- What is the opposite of loud?
- What is the opposite of dry?
- What is the opposite of empty?
- What is the opposite of dark?
- What is the opposite of sad?
- What is the opposite of friend?
- What is the opposite of hate?

The next time you get stressed out, scared, or upset, take some time to sit quietly in front of your Christmas tree. Take some deep breaths while you look at the lights, and imagine Jesus making everything new in heaven.

PRAY

Pray and ask Jesus to help you trust and hope in Him. Give thanks to Jesus for bringing peace.

Love

Feelings follow Actions

"This is my command: Love one another as I have loved you. No one has greater love than this: to lay down his life for his friends."

John 15:12-13

Love is what anchors us to God. It is at the heart of who God is (1 John 4:8) and how He relates to us, His children created in His image. As the apostle John wrote in his Gospel, "For God loved the world in this way: He gave his one and only Son, so that everyone who believes in him will not perish but have eternal life" (John 3:16). Jesus's first advent was God's love on display, and His second one will be no less.

You are made in love by love For love

It is appropriate that we close our Advent study by considering the wonder of God's love, because it undergirds the other three themes—hope, joy, and peace. A day is coming when because of God's great love for us, our hope, joy, and peace will be complete (1 Cor. 13). The Bible passages that wrap up our study this week remind us that God's love for us is seen most clearly in Jesus, and we are to love others as He loves us.

DAY ONE	God's faithful love endures forever (Ps. 118).
DAY TWO	Jesus's birth is the love of God on display (John 1:1-14).
DAY THREE	The love of Jesus changes lives (Luke 7:36-50).
DAY FOUR	Jesus's love for us shapes our love for others (John 15:12-17).
DAY FIVE	Love conquers all (Rev. 21–22).

SILENT NIGHT

Silent night, holy night
All is calm, all is bright
'Round yon virgin mother and Child
Holy infant so tender and mild
Sleep in heavenly peace
Sleep in heavenly peace

Silent night, holy night!
Shepherds quake at the sight!
Glories stream from heaven afar;
Heavenly hosts sing Alleluia!
Christ the Savior is born!
Christ the Savior is born!

Silent night, holy night
Son of God, oh, love's pure light
Radiant beams from Thy holy face
With the dawn of redeeming grace
Jesus, Lord at Thy birth
Jesus, Lord at Thy birth'

WATCH THE VIDEO "Session Four: Love" (15:17) and use the space below to take notes.

HYMN: Silent Night

SCRIPTURE READING: John 1:1-14

Love is an action.

Don't just talk about it – but do it
like get down & play with Kids

Love Surrenders – love summitts!

TO ACCESS THE VIDEO SESSIONS,
USE THE INSTRUCTIONS IN THE BACK OF YOUR BIBLE STUDY BOOK.

Discuss

If you are part of a *The Wonder of Advent* Bible study group, use this page to take notes during your group time and to keep a record of prayer requests that are mentioned.

Day 1

GOD'S LOVE ENDURES FOREVER
PSALM 118

by Joy Allmond

Think about a time when you were overwhelmingly happy to be reunited with someone. Perhaps a loved one returned from a military deployment, or you got to see your beloved new grandbaby after a time away. Or maybe it was when you were reunited with friends or family after being away at college, or the first time your college-age child returned home on break. Think about the joy you felt the first time you were able to see and embrace that person after an extended time away from them. Recall some of the thoughts that went through your head.

I didn't realize how much I missed them.

I can hardly believe we're finally together again!

At last.

It's also safe to say you felt a strong measure of gratitude as you were reminded of how much that person means to you and the love you have for one another. As we begin this last week of the Advent season and read Psalm 118 together, we shift our focus to the theme of God's love. Love is the motivation for everything God has done for us, and His faithful love for His people is the thread that runs through all of Scripture, from the garden to the incarnation to the promise of Jesus's return.

MEMORY VERSE

This is my command: Love one another as I have loved you. No one has greater love than this: to lay down his life for his friends.

John 15:12-13

READ PSALM 118:1-7.

Like with our relatives after an extended time apart, the psalmist is grateful for the presence of the Lord—our triumphant King. When I read through these verses, it's as though I "hear" a tone of relief in the voice of the writer.

What are the key attributes of God the psalmist mentions in verse 1?

The psalmist praised the Lord for who He is and for what He has done. In verse 1 alone, we see evidence that God is good, faithful, loving, and steadfast. The refrain that will echo through this entire psalm of gratitude is, "His faithful love endures forever."

How does the psalmist describe the Lord's actions in verses 5-7? List the key words and phrases from these verses.

The psalmist draws a connection between God's attributes (vv. 1-4) and His actions (vv. 5-7). Think about your own life: How have you seen God's goodness or love reflected in the way He has worked in your life recently?

In verses 5-8, the jubilation is felt as we read these celebratory lines from a weary person who found rest in the faithful love of God. This psalm is part of the Egyptian Hallel (Pss. 113–118), which is a group of psalms the Jews sang at Passover and other annual celebrations.[2] At its heart is God's rescue of His people, likely with the backstory of the Egyptian exodus in mind. But verse 5 also makes it clear the psalmist experienced God's faithfulness and rescue on a very personal level.

Can you identify with that person? How so?

Know that you not only have a Rescuer; you have a Father, and His love endures forever.

READ PSALM 118:8-18.

This looks like testimony time to me! In this next set of verses, the psalmist testified to all the Lord has done. Again, we see a mix of what has been done in the individual's life, and also among a community of people.

This gives me pause: Do I take the time to celebrate what the Lord has done in the lives of other people, like my family or my church community? Do I pay attention to the triumph in others' lives?

What about you? Do you take the time to celebrate God's work in the lives of the people around you? Why is that something we should do?

Of all the listed praises in verses 8-18 regarding what God has done, which one from this passage resonates with you most? Why is it important to you?

Grateful people are the most effective heralds for good news. The psalmist made his delight known. I can almost see him celebrating in the street as he's saying these words! In verse 14 we read, "The LORD is my strength and my song; he has become my salvation." The psalmist and the nation of Israel experienced the Lord's deliverance first-hand, and if you are a follower of Christ, then you have too. Jesus is our strength and our song, and He is our salvation.

> What are you most grateful for when it comes to the work of Jesus and your relationship with Him? Put that into words in the space provided.

This week, identify an area of your life where you've seen great victory and share that with someone else. You never know how you're influencing their eyes to be watchful for the conquering King, our Rescuer.

READ PSALM 118:19-29.

This psalm began by praising God for His faithful love, which endures forever. The psalmist recalled specific ways he experienced God's love in his life. With the verses we just read, the psalm also looks ahead to a future deliverance as more evidence of God's faithful love.

> In the midst of all these praises, what is the one thing the psalmist asked for?

The psalmist sought and received God's salvation (vv. 19,21,25). While this was likely a praise for physical salvation from his enemies, these verses also point us forward to the ultimate act of God's salvation—the sending of His Son. God's saving, enduring love is seen most clearly through Jesus (the cornerstone, v. 22). References to Psalm 118 appear throughout the Gospels in relation to Jesus and His redemptive work, which was motivated by the Father's love. (See Matt. 21:6-11.)

Observing what the Lord has done in our lives as well as others' lives, like the psalmist did here, reminds us we can pray boldly for God to act. What is one bold prayer you want to pray today? Write it here. You may even want to share it with someone else who can join you in boldly approaching the Lord.

"His faithful love endures forever," which we see repeated a few times at the beginning of this passage, resurfaces in verse 29 to close out the psalm. Why is that phrase the perfect ending to this psalm?

Are you hopeful about the future? All the earthly forecasts out there seem dim. Do you ever find it hard to muster up the courage to pray those "longshot" prayers—the ones that, when voiced out loud, almost seem silly? This psalm reminds us that we have a King who conquered death by crucifixion. It's easy to lose sight of that when we struggle with doubt or the same pattern of defeat.

The world had been waiting for a Rescuer. A Savior. A Victor. They needed someone to free captives, heal the sick, and tend to the hearts of the downtrodden. As we also hang in the tension here on earth between the two advents of Jesus, may we take the cues from Psalm 118 to observe and note God's qualities, call out the victories we see in the lives of those around us, and look through a hopeful lens as we boldly pray for Him to work. He is coming again. ★

Day 2

THE WORD BECAME FLESH
JOHN 1:1-14
by Mary Wiley

In the defining moments of my life, the presence of others has been the sweetest gift of love. At twelve, I lost my dad to cancer. When the emotion became overwhelming the night of the visitation, my favorite babysitter took me home and sat with me in my grief.

As a freshman in college, I had a terrible car accident that kept me at my family's home for a few weeks before I could return to school. My friends drove three hours to my home to spend a day with me. They didn't come with quick fixes or medical expertise, but their presence made all the difference.

As a new parent to a sweet adopted baby boy, we were tired and needy. Our church brought meals and spent time with us, calming our brand-new parent anxiety with the wisdom they shared in those moments.

In what ways have you felt most loved?

Through the joys and struggles of life, the greatest vision of love has been the willingness of others to come to me, take off their coats, and stay a while. And yet, this is only a dim reflection of the love Jesus showed when He came to dwell with His people.

READ JOHN 1:1-5.

John 1 and Genesis 1 begin similarly. These prologues lay the theological foundation for the truths that follow. Genesis 1:1 says, "In the beginning God created the heavens and the earth," establishing God's eternality, love, and authority as Creator over all. Similarly, John 1 begins with a proclamation of what was true in the beginning.

John doesn't begin his Gospel with a birth narrative. The story of Jesus's birth is not even mentioned in this Gospel. However, it does begin with a sort of origin story. John affirms that "the Word" was in the beginning, was with God, and was God.

Word in verse 1 is the word *logos* in Greek. *Lexham Bible Dictionary* defines its three uses in the more than three hundred instances in the New Testament as:

1. a message or speech (or the act of speaking);

2. the special revelation of God (or the gospel message that brings salvation);

3. the Person of that revelation: Jesus.[3]

Jesus is the visible message of God. As the Son of God, one part of the Trinity, He is both God and has always existed with God. He was sent to us in love to reveal the depth of God's love for humanity. While on earth, He lived the sinless life we could not live and died to pay for sin and make a way for us to be made right with God. Jesus is the Logos in all three ways.

SKIM GENESIS 1, THEN READ JOHN 1:3-5 AGAIN. How do John's verses echo the creation account from Genesis 1?

Jesus is not just the giver of life and light; He is life and light. He is the source of all life and light we know today. This is both biological and spiritual, as He is the agent of creation and the agent of recreation—our new life found in Him. These gifts are the outworking of His love.

What attributes presented in this passage can you praise Jesus for? How might you need to respond to Him today?

READ JOHN 1:6-9. What does this passage reveal about John the Baptist's purpose?

This aside about John the Baptist seems like a strange interruption in chapter 1, but John (the author) knew what he was doing. Many in his audience thought John the Baptist might be the Messiah, and they rejected Jesus. He needed to capture their attention quickly so that he could make clear the truth about the true Messiah, Jesus.

The imagery used to describe John is that of a herald or witness sent home ahead of a victorious king after battle. The herald would call the people into the streets to celebrate their king for his success and for protecting all under his rule. John the Baptist was the one excitedly yelling in the streets, not the Defeater of enemies and the Provider of peace.

What might it look like for you to be a bold herald for Jesus, following John the Baptist's example?

READ JOHN 1:10-14.

The heralded King would not be recognized by His people; the creation would be blind to the Creator. He "came to his own"—or what may be translated as "he came home"—and was not received. Despite knowing this would be His reception, in love, Jesus came anyway.

Why do you think so many who had waited on the Messiah to come for centuries did not recognize Him when He finally arrived?

For many Jews, their understanding of God was so lofty they couldn't fathom a lowly, gentle Savior, born in a stable. For many Greeks, the gods were too limited to be the one true God; instead they were like Zeus or Hermes, deities packed with vices. Yet, John says Jesus is better than both perspectives: He is fully God and fully man: eternal, authoritative, gentle, and powerful, and He has come near.

> In your Bible, circle the conjunction that begins verse 12, or write it here: _____.

Verse 12 is the good news of the gospel! Through Christ, we have been grafted into the family of God as rightful children and heirs. Love drove Him to become a human being and to become family with us in all our maladies.

> Write John 1:14 below.

> Circle the actions of the Word. Put a square around what those who gazed upon Christ might observe and underline its two describing words. *Becoming flesh + being among us!*

The word "dwelt" could also be translated "dwelt as in a tent among us."[4] Jesus is a picture of the tabernacle, the tent pitched where God's presence dwelled with His people as they traveled toward the promised land (Ex. 26). There, God's people met with Him, atoned for sin, and worshiped. Through Christ, we have access to the Father, atonement for sin, and may worship in His presence! Jesus has torn the veil separating God's people from His holy presence. In love, He draws us back into the holy presence of God.

> If God has come near through Christ, what does that mean for our lives today? How might it affect the way you think about God, pray, and seek Him? *More personal*
>
> *Observing the Glory - Grace & Truth*

Nothing can separate you from the love of Christ. He has taken on flesh and dwelled among us. May we get lost in the glory of His incarnation as we reflect on Him today. Spend some time thanking God for His great love that would send His Son to dwell among us and make a way to be made right with Him again. He could have saved His people in a thousand other ways, but He chose nearness. Presence.

In love, God made a way for us to be with Him both today and forever. Love marked His coming to be with us; love marked His way to the cross on our behalf; and love will mark His return. ★

WONDERS OF HIS LOVE
LUKE 7:36-50

by Jessica Yentzer

One of my favorite Christmas Eve traditions is attending a church service where we sing carols and read Scripture about Jesus's birth. It's one of the few moments each year when I can count on the bustle of activity to slow, the buzz of my anxious thoughts to grow quiet, and the full weight of Jesus's first coming to sink in. One of my favorite songs we sing is "Joy to the World," and when I read today's passage, the final verse of the song came to mind:

> *He rules the world with truth and grace*
>
> *and makes the nations prove*
>
> *the glories of his righteousness*
>
> *and wonders of his love.*

As we dive into the story of a woman who anointed Jesus's feet, we'll see her act of love was inspired by wonder for the God who saw her, knew her, and loved her.

READ LUKE 7:36-38.

What do these verses tell us about the woman who anointed Jesus's feet?

When I'm reading Scripture, I'm always struck by which details make it into a narrative account. Luke doesn't tell us a name, a physical description, or really any details at all about the woman who entered the Pharisee's house to see Jesus. We simply learn that she was a sinner. What a humbling detail to serve as her identity as this story begins.

What stands out to you about the way the woman interacted with Jesus?

Each time I read these verses, something new stands out about this woman and the way she demonstrated her love for Jesus. First, I see her humility as she wiped His feet with her hair—feet that were likely dirty from walking along dusty roads. Then, I see her overflowing gratitude and love as she wept at Jesus's feet, kissed them, and anointed Him with expensive perfume. And lastly, I see her boldness in coming to the Pharisee's house to begin with—uninvited. I can only imagine the judgment she knew she was opening herself up to by showing up that day. Jesus's presence compelled her to action, almost as if she couldn't stay away from the One who saw her and loved her, sins and all. Let's keep going in our story.

READ LUKE 7:39-43. How did the Pharisee respond to the woman's actions?

In verse 39, we get to hear a bit of Simon the Pharisee's inner monologue as he processed what unfolded in front of him. He was filled with disdain for this sinful woman who touched Jesus. But what I find most interesting are his thoughts about Jesus: "This man, if he were a prophet, would know who and what kind of woman this is . . ." Simon's statement revealed he was a skeptic at best, but Luke reminds us he shouldn't have been. Jesus demonstrated His divine power to know the heart and mind in His response to Simon.

Don't you love that Jesus addressed Simon's disdain with a story? We see Jesus do this throughout the Gospels, offering parables and stories to answer questions and teach His disciples, the Pharisees, and the crowds.

In your own words, what was the main point of the parable Jesus told Simon?

When was the last time you reflected on how much you've been forgiven? Write out a statement of praise to God for the debts He's forgiven for you.

It can be easy to lose sight of the weight of our sin as we get caught up in our day-to-day lives. And even when we acknowledge our sinfulness, how often do we try to soften the blow as we bring those weaknesses to God? There have certainly been seasons in my life when confession was difficult and bringing the specifics of my sin to the Lord was not easy. But the more clearly we're able to see the vastness of our sinful hearts, the better our vantage point to see the depth of God's grace and love for us.

READ LUKE 7:44-50.

In the chart below, record the contrasts Jesus makes between the woman and Simon.

SIMON	THE WOMAN

Why did the woman love so much? Why did Simon love so little?

In verse 47, Jesus said, "Therefore I tell you, her many sins have been forgiven; that's why she loved much. But the one who is forgiven little, loves little."

I wish we had another glimpse inside Simon's head as he heard those words. Was Simon confused by what Jesus said? Did it offend or anger him? Or was he convicted by Jesus's call for him to examine his own heart—to see his sin and how much he had been forgiven? The CSB Study Bible notes, "Jesus did not mean that the Pharisee had little sin to be forgiven but that he did not think of himself as a sinner while the woman was profoundly aware of her sinfulness."[5] We are all sinners who have been forgiven much (Rom. 3:23).

This woman we met as a sinner is now known to us as forgiven. She understood the change Jesus brought to her life, and that prompted an overflow of love from her. When we grow in our knowledge and perspective of God's love, it naturally prompts a response of love and praise from us. We are filled with awe and wonder at His love just like the woman who washed and anointed Jesus's feet.

How can you keep your eyes fixed on the wonder of God's love this season? Write down two to three practical ways to remind yourself of His love for you. (This could look like memorizing Scripture about God's love, spending time in prayer praising God for His love and grace, and more.) ★

Day 4

AS I HAVE LOVED YOU
JOHN 15:9-17

by Lynley Mandrell

In the book *Life Together*, Dietrich Bonhoeffer wrote: "The person who loves their dream of community will destroy community, but the person who loves those around them will create community."[6] Within the local church, I have seen this quote effectively used by pastors many times. It is a go-to when the love is running low in the pews. Christians need to be challenged to keep on loving their spiritual siblings—to keep on forgiving. Love is the glue that holds the church together.

And yet, with holiday gatherings approaching, Bonhoeffer's words could be modified to bring us a fresh challenge in our homes as well: "The person who loves their dream of family will destroy the family, but the person who loves those around them will create family."

The true test of Christianity comes down to this, doesn't it? Love is what holds it all together.

READ JOHN 15:9-17.

How many times does Jesus say "love" or "loved" in this passage?

———

In this passage from John's Gospel, which my Bible titles "Christlike love," Jesus uses a form of the word *love* nine times. The previous verses in John (1-8), which we studied in Week Two, described a relationship to God as abiding in Him, like branches connected to their vine. Here we see that the way we stay connected to Jesus is through loving obedience to Him.

LOOK CLOSER AT VERSE 12. If love is a command, what does that mean for the follower of Christ?

In verse 12 we read, "This is my command: Love one another as I have loved you." Notice, he didn't say, "This is my suggestion." It's a clear command, with no room for appeal. What Jesus expects from you this Christmas is your renewed commitment to love. For Jesus, the ultimate demonstration of His love was His sacrificial death on the cross. For us, it looks more like constant, relentless, sacrificial acts, putting others before ourselves, and doing whatever it takes to make sure people see the love of Jesus through us.

As we consider Christ's call to love this Christmas, I want to draw out two points from this convicting passage.

1. Jesus talks the talk and walks the walk.

The highest form of love comes with the highest form of sacrifice. There is no greater love than this: to lay down your life for a friend. With the full New Testament in our hands, we have the advantage of hindsight. We can see so many things the disciples couldn't, namely, the crucifixion.

Jesus taught them that love is truly defined by the measure of pain one is willing to endure for the other. As He spoke those words, He must have seen in His mind the nails, the thorns, the spears, the Roman soldiers. He knew exactly what the excruciating days ahead would involve, and love alone motivated Him to move forward.

In the space provided, write out a paraphrase of verse 12.

If you are to love as Jesus loves, what does that look like?

The disciples thought they were hearing a poetic description of love, but instead, they were hearing a plan for how Jesus would show His love. It's a game plan for our lives as well. Painful sacrifice is the key to growing closer to others. It is the key to growing closer to God.

My husband, Ben, and I have been married for twenty-one years. You would think that the longer we've been married, the easier it would be to love each other. That has not been the case. We've experienced more trials in the last three years than all the previous years combined. In this season, we've had to actively and consciously choose to work it out and love the other. It hasn't been easy, but that's the way Jesus's idea of love works.

The euphoric feelings that followed our wedding vows were special but short-lived. Building a strong relationship requires day-after-day sacrifice. It demands work. Like Jesus, we have to walk the walk.

> Think of a relationship that is asking extra sacrifice from you these days. What has made it hard to love that person? What would it look like for you to love like Jesus in that specific relationship?

2. Jesus connects friendship with obedience.

In a day when many people point to church attendance to prove they are true Christians, Jesus points to something else: obedience. The willingness to do exactly what Jesus tells us to do even when it hurts. Especially when it hurts.

Peter was listening. Jesus's words were exactly what he wanted to hear, and he was primed and ready to go to the grave for his master if that's what the job required. Until it actually required it.

> READ JOHN 18:15-18. Write down three observations you have as you read through these verses.

Peter had heard Jesus's teaching about love, obedience, and friendship. But as Peter watched Jesus suffer and feared what could happen to him by association, he denied even knowing Jesus, let alone serving Him. Peter called himself a friend, but in Jesus's hour of greatest need Peter's self-preservation kicked in. Obedience was too tall of an order.

Just like Peter, all of us want to turn and run when love asks too much of us. Yet, in these moments of testing we truly learn what it means to follow Jesus, and what great rewards are on the other side of obedience.

So, what does all this mean to you? In this Advent season, as you consider Christ's call to love, where do you feel most challenged? If you're drawing a blank, let me suggest two practical lists you might make, as a worshipful exercise.

> First, make a list of people in your life who feel impossible to love. Keep that list close until Christmas, committing to pray for those individuals.

Bonhoeffer helps us one more time: "I can no longer condemn, or hate a brother for whom I pray, no matter how much trouble he causes me."[7]

> Second, make a list of the loyal people in your life.

For some reason, the human eye is drawn to what is off, broken, or wrong in the world. There is so much right, and there are so many blessings. All around you, God has placed people who watch your back, who speak well of your name, who light up when they see you. People who love you like Jesus does. They are called friends. Whether you recognize it or not, they are the greatest gifts on planet earth.

James reminds us that every good and perfect gift comes from the Father above (Jas. 1:17). As you commit this Christmas to pray for those who have hurt you, be sure to praise God for those who have helped you and made many sacrifices to show you that you are loved. Because you are. ★

Day 5

LOVE CONQUERS ALL
REVELATION 21–22
by Amanda Mejias

Before we begin our final day's study, take a few minutes to reflect on your life and the current state of the world over this past year.

List five words you would use to describe this past year of your life.

1.

2.

3.

4.

5.

List five significant events that happened in the world around you.

1.

2.

3.

4.

5.

What were some of the greatest joys you experienced?

What were the hardest trials you encountered?

How did you see God's love impact your life this year?

As you reflected over the highs and lows of this year, my prayer is that you were overwhelmed with gratitude for the grace and love God demonstrated to you through it all. No matter how thankful you might be about how the Lord showed up for you, though, I know it doesn't negate the pain of the trials you faced or take away the immense suffering you witnessed in the world around you.

A question we often hear (or even ask ourselves) is, *How can God's love be so good, yet our world be so broken?* When our lives are marked by grief, heartache, suffering, and regret, it's our flesh's response to immediately question the love of God. And while this wrestling is completely normal, it's important for us to not leave it at that. We must remind ourselves that this is not the life or the world God created or desired for us.

In the very beginning of Genesis, Adam and Eve were in the garden experiencing the world as whole and good. Not only did they walk around in a perfect world, but they walked with God Himself. His presence was tangible to Adam and Eve. He knew them. They knew His face. But before long, sin entered the world, and then what had been created good and whole was shattered.

   READ GENESIS 3:6-24. Why were Adam and Eve hiding from God?

What were the immediate consequences of their sin?

I don't know about you, but when I think about the impact of Adam's and Eve's sin, I often think about verses 14-19 with the labor pains and the cursed ground, consequences we feel on the daily. But what I often forget as the greatest consequence to their sin was a broken relationship with their Creator. Can you imagine being Adam and Eve the day when God not only removed them from the garden but removed them from His presence?

Can you pinpoint a time when you felt far from the presence of God? How do you think Adam and Eve felt on that day?

Adam and Eve—and all humans—were created to bring glory to God and to be in relationship with Him, but their sin removed them from seeing the face of their Creator, from communing with Him, and from experiencing the life they were created to live.

But God.

READ EPHESIANS 2:1-5.

Paul described the way you and I lived before following Jesus as being dead in our sin. What does this description communicate to you?

Why is it important to understand who you are apart from God's salvation?

What were the motivating factors of God in moving us from death to life (Eph. 2:4-5)?

Friends, God could have left us dead in our sin. He could have wiped His hands clean and started a new world with new people to love. Thankfully, our God is a God of love. Therefore, He made a way for us to not only be set free from our sin, but a way that we could have a relationship with Him and experience His presence once again.

But wait, it gets better! God doesn't just want a relationship with us now, where we experience His presence among the brokenness of this world. God is going to make all things new, so we can experience the relationship He intended to have with humanity from the very beginning.

Revelation 21–22 is a beautiful picture of the new heaven and new earth. Imagine a world without death, grief, sorrow, or pain as seen in Revelation 21:4. My heart longs for that day. But experiencing the new heaven isn't just about what we won't have to worry about anymore; it's about what we gain, too.

READ REVELATION 22:1-4.

What is different in these verses from what you read earlier in Genesis 3?

There will be no more curse! The tree of life that once led to death will lead to life and healing. And because there will be no more sin and no more curse, we will finally be able to experience the presence of God fully as intended from the beginning of Genesis. His love for us will come full circle as we will be invited to not just know Him, but to see His face.

Sit for a minute and try to imagine what that will be like. Journal what your response might be to finally seeing God face-to-face for the first time.

This broken world doesn't leave us full of hope or eager expectations most days. As we often drift from one struggle to the next, the concepts of hope and peace feel distant. But what anchors us back is to know the same God who loved us enough to create us and to have a relationship with us is the same God who has promised to make all things new, to redeem what sin destroyed, and to offer us full, face-to-face access to Him one day.

When our hearts are set on that side of His perfect, redemptive love, we can be like Paul in Romans 8:18 and proclaim, "For I consider that the sufferings of this present time are not worth comparing with the glory that is going to be revealed to us." Amen, come Lord Jesus! ★

HOW TO MAKE A CHRISTMAS HOST TRAY

by Chelsea Waack

On the fourth week of Advent, you can almost reach out and touch Christmas. While you've been preparing your heart for weeks, it's now time to prepare gifts for loved ones. Combine useful, everyday items with festive ribbon and evergreen clippings to create a gift that will make any host feel loved.

SUPPLIES

- Wooden tray
- Christmas tea towel
- Wooden spoon
- Ribbon or twine
- Pine clippings
- Thank you card with an envelope
- Pen
- Clear tape

DIRECTIONS

1. Write a short thank you note for your host, seal it in an envelope with their name on it, and set aside.

2. Assemble the contents of your tray. Place a tea towel on the tray. Secure the card to the center of the tea towel with a loop of clear tape. Then, place the wooden spoon on top.

3. Wrap ribbon around the entire contents of the tray. Before you tighten the ribbon, add in pine clippings on either side of the spoon. Finish by tying a bow around the spoon's handle.

4. Bring to your Christmas gathering to surprise and delight your host.

> **TIP**
>
> This gift is completely customizable. The wooden tray could be substituted for a basket or cutting board. Other fun options would be to include a rolling pin, tapered candles, or a bag of coffee.